Contents

Acknowledgements	ix
List of illustrations	xi

Chapter 1 Global Citizenship, and why it is important in schools — 1

The 'what' and the 'why' of Global Citizenship

What is Global Citizenship?	1
Elements of Global Citizenship	2
Global Citizenship and the curriculum	2
Global Citizenship and Development Education	2
Background to the Handbook	4
The role of Global Citizenship in education	5
Finally ... addressing concerns	7
References	9

Chapter 2 Global Citizenship in the whole school — 11

Suggestions on how to implement Global Citizenship through a whole-school approach

Developing understanding of Global Citizenship: whole-school in-service activities	11
Theme *What is a Global Citizen?*	12
Theme *'Contentious' issues*	15
Theme *Presenting positive images in work with people, places and artefacts*	20
Theme *Presenting positive images through using artefacts*	22
Theme *Presenting positive images through promoting critical thinking: 'Bias Alert!' – a look at multimedia resources*	23
Theme *Sustainable development*	26
Theme *Linking with the community – welcoming visitors*	29

Global Citizenship: The Handbook for Primary Teaching

Whole-school audit	**31**
Examples of good practice in Global Citizenship	*33*
Mission statement	33
Providing a supportive environment and raising self-esteem	33
Effective Equal Opportunities policy	33
Behaviour management	34
Democratic and inclusive processes	34
Variety of teaching methods	34
Whole-school Global Citizenship initiatives and events	35
Governing bodies / school boards	36
Ethical practices	36
Learning from people from diverse backgrounds and from around the world	36
Commitment to sustainable development	37
Resources and displays	38
The wider community	38
Support for staff	39
References	*39*

Chapter 3 Activities to bring Global Citizenship into your school — 41

Assembly ideas and classroom activities to explore issues of Global Citizenship across the primary curriculum

Assemblies	**44**
Brief assembly ideas for Global Citizenship themes	*44*
Social justice and equity	44
Globalisation and interdependence	45
Appreciation of diversity	45
Sustainable development	46
Peace and conflict resolution	46
Local and global news	*47*
A Global Citizenship assembly calendar	*48*
Classroom activities	**52**
Using the activities	*52*
The Global Citizenship curriculum outline	*52*
Foundation Stage (England), Pre-5 (Scotland)/Early Years (Wales)	**59**
Social justice and equity	59
Globalisation and interdependence	60
Appreciation of diversity	62
Sustainable development	63
Peace and conflict resolution	66
KS1 (England and Wales), P1–P3 (Scotland)	**67**
Social justice and equity	67
Globalisation and interdependence	69
Appreciation of diversity	71
Sustainable development	75
Peace and conflict resolution	78

KS2 (England and Wales), P4–P7 (Scotland)	**81**
A note about simulation games	*81*
Social justice and equity	81
Globalisation and interdependence	85
Appreciation of diversity	92
Sustainable development	97
Peace and conflict resolution	102
References	*104*

Chapter 4 Global Citizenship and Literacy — 105

Three sets of lessons for three different age groups on the themes of bullying, children's rights and Nelson Mandela

Bullying	**106**
Learning objectives	*106*
Comprehension and composition (text-level work)	107
Grammar and punctuation (sentence-level work)	109
Spelling and vocabulary (word-level work)	110
Children's rights	**117**
Learning objectives	*117*
Comprehension and composition (text-level work)	119
Nelson Mandela: biography and autobiography	**132**
Learning objectives	*132*
Text-level work	133
References	*155*

Chapter 5 Global Citizenship and Geography — 157

Pointers on teaching Geography in a way that promotes Global Citizenship

Maps	**158**
School linking	**160**
Teaching about distant localities	**161**
Unit 1 Around our school – the local area	162
Unit 5 Where in the world is Barnaby Bear?	162
Unit 7 Weather around the world	164
Unit 8 Improving the environment	164
Unit 10 A village in India	165
Unit 11 Water	165
Unit 16 What's in the news?	166
Unit 17 Global eye	167
Unit 20 Local traffic – an environmental issue	168
Unit 22 A contrasting locality overseas – Tocuaro	169
Unit 24 Passport to the world	170
References	*172*

Chapter 6 Resources and contacts — 173

A selected list of children's books, resource books and contacts to help you take the issues forward

Children's books — 174
- Social justice and equity — 174
- Globalisation and interdependence — 175
- Appreciation of diversity — 176
- Sustainable development — 177
- Peace and conflict resolution — 178

Resources for teachers — 179
- Social justice and equity — 179
- Globalisation and interdependence — 180
- Appreciation of diversity — 181
- Sustainable development — 181
- Peace and conflict resolution — 182
- Books for initial teacher education — 183
- Whole-school resources — 183
- Periodicals and newsletters — 183

Contacts — 184
- Additional support for Citizenship in primary schools — 187
- Development Education Centres — 187

Acknowledgements

The publishers are grateful to the following organisations for their permission to use copyright material in this Handbook. Whilst every effort has been made to trace and acknowledge ownership of copyright, the publishers will be glad to make suitable arrangements with any copyright holders whom it has not been possible to contact. The authors are grateful to all individuals and organisations not listed on this page, but acknowledged in the text, who have granted permission for their work to be used.

Extract of *Charles's Story* taken from *It's Our Right*, published by Save the Children in association with UNICEF/UK, 1990.

Extract of *Daring to be a Teacher*, by Robin Richardson, published by Trentham Books, 1990, reproduced with permission.

Extract of *Nelson Mandela*, by Benjamin Pogrund © Exley Publications.

pp. 5–8 from *Nelson Mandela: A Biography* by Martin Meredith (Hamish Hamilton, 1997) © Martin Meredith, 1997. Reproduced by permission of Penguin Books Ltd.

Extract of *Talking Rights: Taking Responsibility*, used by permission of UNICEF, www.unicef.org.uk/education/citizenship

Extracts from *Long Walk to Freedom* by Nelson Mandela. ©1994 by Nelson Rolihlahla Mandela. By permission of Little, Brown and Company (Inc.).

Quotation from Liam O'Neill in *Stand Up for Your Rights* by Peace Child International (1988), Two-Can Publishing, reproduced with permission.

Text from *For Every Child* by UNICEF published by Hutchinson. Used by permission of the Random House Group Limited.

Illustration, *The Two Mules*, used by permission of Quaker Peace & Social Witness.

Extract from *Primary Values: A Literacy Based Resource for Primary Schools* © 1999, with permission of the Northern Ireland Council for the Curriculum, Examinations and Assessment.

'Dear Teacher' from *Learning from Experience*, ed. Miriam Steiner, published by Trentham Books, 1993, reproduced with permission.

The authors would like to thank the following individuals and organisations for their contributions to the publication

Readers

Christine Dale, Trish Sandbach, Cathy Midwinter, Stephen Scoffham, Lorna Jackson, Chris Godfrey, Annie Clews, Val Rae, Sally Palmer, Fiona Feehan, Annabelle Dixon, Janice Hervieu, Rowena Kerr, Kathy Alcock, Jonathan Barnes, Anna Reid, Etwyn Roberts, Cathie Holden, Stephen Sterling, Margot Brown, Lesley Reader, Eleanor Kercher, Jo Wardally, Leah Elliot

Advice and case studies

Jo Young, Charlie Harvey, Dave Hicks, Peter Barton, Bernie Ashmore, Stuart McLeod, Tara Flood, Heather Jarvis, Rose McCauseland, Matt Parsonage, Marion Walter, Heather Swainston, Margaret Burr, Sharon Ansell, Jane Gregory, Paula Owens, Morag Law, Richard Cupidi, Mara Christie, Michael Arlow, Rob Unwin, Noirin O'Sullivan, Wendy Horden, Caren Brooks, Colin Bridge, Angus Wilson, Angela Latham, Norma Smith, Laura Pratt, Caroline Katiyo, Ros Wade, Louise Douglas, Nicki Donaldson, Katrina Gass

Oxfam Education staff

Penny Justice, Heather King, Catherine Hester, Mary Patience, Anne Kane

Thanks also to the many teachers and children who offered ideas and suggestions during workshops and in-service sessions.

For helping with research, thanks to The Golden Treasury Bookshop, Southfields and Southfields Public Library.

Illustrations

Photos

1	Language Games at Oxfam's Global Citizenship Conference, 2000	37
2	Whitehaven Docks	61
3	Children playing Bagchal	90
4	Miso'shi Fiadogbe-Procter drumming with friends at a school in Cheshire	160
5	Bhavini Algarra from Canterbury DEC helping pupils at Selling School, Kent, set up email links with schools overseas	172

Figures

1	Global Citizenship at primary level	3
2	Traits for the educator aspiring to be a Global Citizen	13
3	The key elements for responsible citizenship	42
4	The Two Mules	46
5	Recipe book	72
6	Timeline	76
7	Sunflowers	79
8	Diamond ranking	84
9	Fairtrade symbol	88
10	Bagchal board	91
11	World Map, centred on the Arctic Circle	158
12	Peters Projection, oriented with east at the top	159

> A Global Citizen doesn't care what race or colour a person is, but cares about how they might feel inside.
>
> *Sheila Birungi, pupil at Sunnyhill Primary School, Streatham, London*

> A Global Citizen should think about the future, respect different cultures and treat others the way they would like to be treated themselves.
>
> *Andrew Coyle, pupil at St Fillan's Primary School, Renfrewshire*

> Our school motto is 'where our children's future matters most'. We exemplify this through our teaching of Global Citizenship – an exciting and welcome addition to the curriculum of humankind – enabling us to extend our vision from the school, to the community to the wider world.
>
> *Lorna Jackson, Headteacher, Maryland Primary School, Stratford, London*

> In Wales great emphasis is placed on cultural identity through the 'Curriculum Cymreig'. Based on this love of their own culture, Welsh children are responsive to all cultures. Global Citizenship helps develop positive and supportive attitudes and gives an understanding of the interdependence of the world and its peoples.
>
> *Morag Law, Deputy Head, Glyncoed Infant and Nursery School, Pentwyn, Cardiff*

> I realise that we must teach children a range of skills (especially related to literacy and to ICT) to help them in their current and future lives. This focus pales into insignificance, however, compared with the need to ask pupils to consider their lives, and the lives of others. The values and attitudes linked to Global Citizenship are clearly the most significant aspects of our work in schools.
>
> *Martin Oldfield, County Adviser for Humanities, Suffolk*

> As we enter the twenty first century and the political, economic and ecological interdependence of nations becomes ever more apparent, we need to reaffirm our priorities. The promotion of Global Citizenship is one of the key issues for the future.
>
> *Stephen Scoffham, Senior Geography Lecturer, Canterbury Christ Church University College, Kent*

> It is only by providing children with the time and opportunity to discuss and think about contentious issues that they'll be able to make informed decisions and act as responsible adults in a global society.
>
> *Gill Silson, Teacher, Ivegill Primary School, Cumbria*

> Global Citizenship is relevant to all National Curriculum subjects but it is a concept that often requires explanation. The Handbook will no doubt establish itself as a useful resource which addresses any preconceptions people may have about Global Citizenship, the uncertainty teachers have as to how to incorporate it into subjects at school, and provides useful contacts for guidance and support.
>
> *Rt Hon Estelle Morris MP, Secretary of State for Education*

Chapter 1
Global Citizenship, and why it is important in schools

What is Global Citizenship?

You may well have come across the notion of 'Global Citizenship', but what does it mean? It is a term being used increasingly in educational circles, and consequently there are a variety of views about what it is. These range from the idea that everyone is a citizen of the globe to the standpoint that in a legal sense there is no such thing as a Global Citizen.

At Oxfam Education, we believe that Global Citizenship is more than the sum of its parts. It goes beyond simply knowing that we are citizens of the globe to an acknowledgement of our responsibilities both to each other and to the Earth itself. Global Citizenship is about understanding the need to tackle injustice and inequality, and having the desire and ability to work actively to do so. It is about valuing the Earth as precious and unique, and safeguarding the future for those coming after us. Global Citizenship is a way of thinking and behaving. It is an outlook on life, a belief that we can make a difference.

We see a Global Citizen as someone who:
- is aware of the wider world and has a sense of their own role as a world citizen
- respects and values diversity
- has an understanding of how the world works economically, politically, socially, culturally, technologically and environmentally
- is outraged by social injustice
- participates in and contributes to the community at a range of levels from local to global
- is willing to act in order to make the world a more equitable and sustainable place
- takes responsibility for their actions.

(Oxfam 1997)

This description of a Global Citizen is the ideal. It may feel like rather a tall order, but don't be put off! Everyone has the potential to be a Global Citizen if they wish to, and is somewhere along the path towards that goal. For those willing to take up the challenge, all you need is courage, commitment, and a sense of humour.

To create a world of Global Citizens, education must be a priority. Global Citizenship is not an additional subject – it is an ethos. It can best be implemented through a whole-school approach, involving everyone with a stake in educating children, from the children themselves to those with teaching and non-teaching roles in the school, parents, governors/school board members, and the wider community.

It can also be promoted in class through teaching the existing curriculum in a way that highlights aspects such as social justice, the appreciation of diversity and the importance of sustainable development.

In the wider school setting, Global Citizenship can be reflected in the way you relate to those around you: it is as much to do with how visitors are welcomed as it is about what and how teachers teach. This is because Global Citizenship in schools is based on the following principles:

- the importance of reaffirming or developing a sense of identity and self-esteem
- valuing all pupils and addressing inequality within and outside school
- acknowledging the importance of relevant values, attitudes, and personal and social education
- willingness to learn from the experiences of others around the world
- relevance to young people's interests and needs
- supporting and increasing young people's motivation to effect change
- a holistic approach to Global Citizenship – that it should be an ethos permeating all areas of school life.

(Oxfam 1997)

These principles apply throughout school life, across all subject areas and within all age groups. We see them as the foundation on which education should be built: as a basic entitlement for all pupils.

Elements of Global Citizenship

Global Citizenship and the curriculum

Global Citizenship is relevant to all curriculum areas in England, Scotland and Wales. Although the subject names and requirements may differ between the three nations, all subjects can be taught through a Global Citizenship approach.

Global Citizenship and Development Education

Oxfam Education's concept of the Global Citizen has grown out of the ideas and principles of Development Education. You may be familiar with Development Education, or with work in related fields such as Education for Sustainable Development, Human Rights Education or the other 'adjectival educations' in the diagram opposite. You may also be wondering how Global Citizenship relates to them.

We see Global Citizenship as an umbrella term, encompassing and developing the issues within the areas of education in the diagram. Each of the areas has useful and interesting materials helpful to those trying to get to grips with aspects of Global Citizenship. In drawing up our definition and principles of Global Citizenship we have been aware of and been inspired by work in these different areas.

We have also included the subject areas for England (E), Scotland (S) and Wales (W) on the diagram. (Those subjects without E, S or W apply to all three.) The diagram shows that through Global Citizenship both curriculum areas and 'adjectival educations' can be integrated.

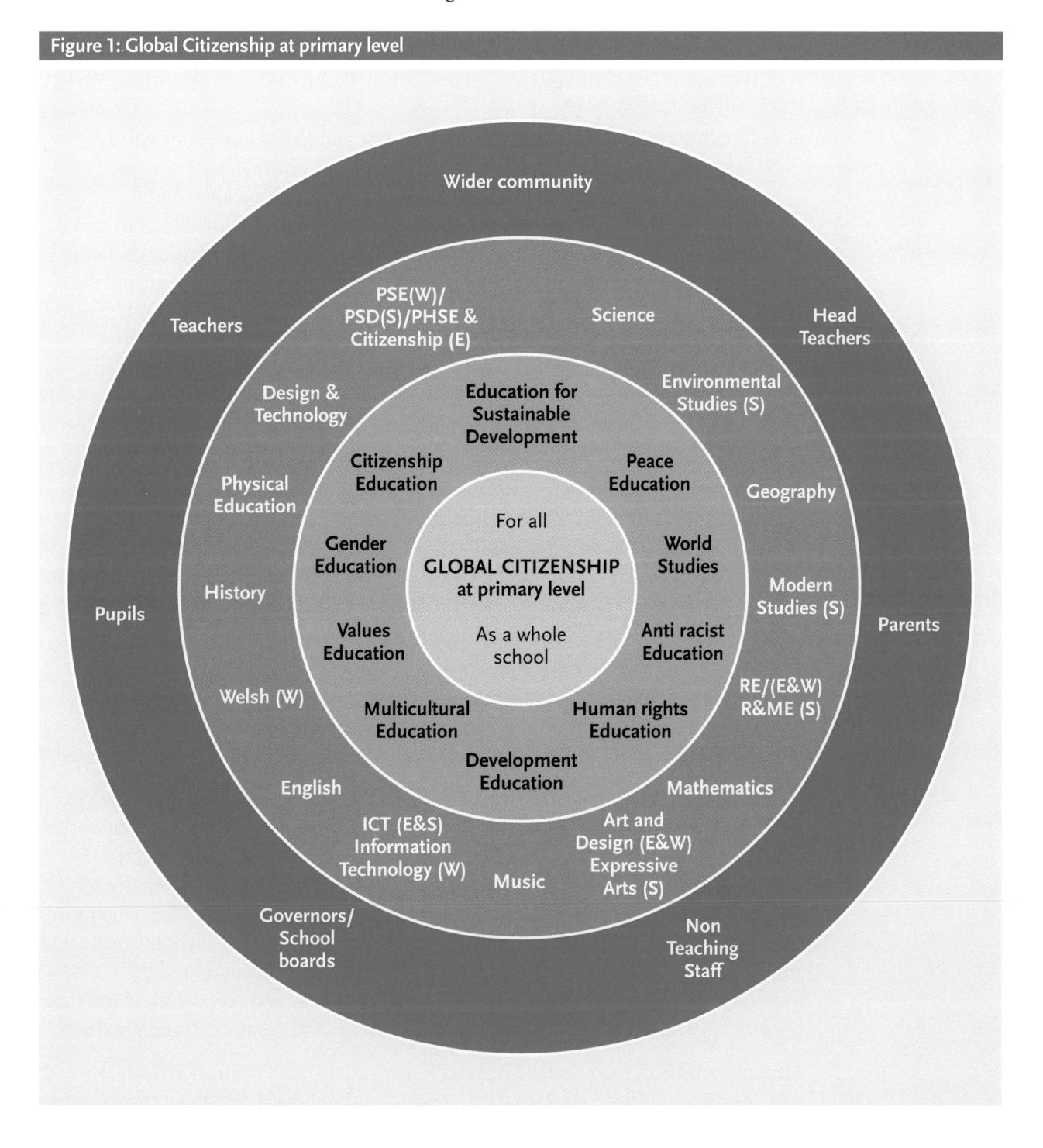

Figure 1: Global Citizenship at primary level

Outer ring (Wider community): Teachers, Head Teachers, Pupils, Parents, Governors/School boards, Non Teaching Staff

Curriculum subjects ring: PSE(W)/PSD(S)/PHSE & Citizenship (E), Science, Design & Technology, Environmental Studies (S), Physical Education, Geography, History, Modern Studies (S), Welsh (W), RE/(E&W) R&ME (S), English, Mathematics, ICT (E&S) Information Technology (W), Music, Art and Design (E&W) Expressive Arts (S)

Adjectival educations ring: Education for Sustainable Development, Citizenship Education, Peace Education, Gender Education, World Studies, Values Education, Anti racist Education, Multicultural Education, Human rights Education, Development Education

Centre: For all GLOBAL CITIZENSHIP at primary level As a whole school

Background to the Handbook

This Handbook expands on our publication, *A Curriculum for Global Citizenship* (Oxfam 1997). This presented our vision of what education should be about if we are to equip children with the knowledge, skills and attitudes to tackle the problems of social injustice and poverty in the world. *A Curriculum for Global Citizenship* has been received well. It has sparked debate among education professionals in the UK and overseas, and has formed the basis of local and international education initiatives.

Public interest in *A Curriculum for Global Citizenship* has been due to a number of factors.

- It has caught the imagination of many educators, who see it as idealistic, but also sensible and achievable.

- Its publication coincided with a renewed interest in global issues in England, Wales and Scotland. This was generated in England by the Department for International Development (DfID), the Department for Education and Employment (DfEE) (now the DfES) and the Development Education movement. One result was a collaboration by the DfEE, DfID, the Qualifications and Curriculum Authority (QCA), the Development Education Association and the Central Bureau, to produce guidance for schools in England entitled *Developing a Global Dimension in the School Curriculum* (2000). In Scotland, Learning and Teaching Scotland published *The Global Dimension in the Curriculum* (2001), a collaboration between DfID, the Scottish Executive and the International Development Education Association of Scotland (IDEAS). This guidance has been sent to all schools in Scotland. Plans are afoot for a similar publication for Wales.

- Citizenship and PSHE were included in the English curriculum, and PSE in the Welsh curriculum, for the first time from September 2000 (albeit as a non-statutory subject at primary level). Oxfam Education's Global Citizenship learning outcomes informed the Citizenship and PSHE guidelines for schools in England and the PSE framework in Wales. Many educators can see the links between Global Citizenship and Citizenship and PSHE/ PSE/ PSD more clearly than in other areas of the curriculum.

- It presents a practical way of working towards tackling racism in society, as highlighted as a priority in the *MacPherson Report* (1999) into the murder of Stephen Lawrence.

In considering issues of Global Citizenship, we acknowledge that we have much to learn from others around the world. This is especially true of the Majority World countries (those sometimes described as 'developing') which, in general, consume considerably less of the world's resources than those in the Minority World (or so-called 'developed' countries). Those of us who consume most are the ones who most need to examine our lifestyles. It is also important to acknowledge technological advantages. For instance, this Handbook has been written utilising modern technology from a comfortable room. This is a rather easy and very detached position from which to discuss issues of poverty and injustice, and the need to address them.

Although this Handbook is for English, Welsh and Scottish primary schools, we feel that an education based on Global Citizenship is of universal relevance. These words from Kofi Annan, the Director General of the UN, reflect this:

> **❝** To look into some aspects of the future we do not need projections by supercomputers. Much of the next millennium can be seen in how we care for pupils today. Tomorrow's world may be influenced by science and technology but more than anything, it is already taking shape in the bodies and minds of our pupils. **❞**
>
> *('Why make a special case for children?' www.unicef.org/crc/specialcase 14/05/01)*

The role of Global Citizenship in education

> **❝** Global Citizenship reflects what we want to do and what we believe – it's how children develop and grow. **❞**
>
> *Mara Chrystie, Head Teacher at Hermitage Primary School, London*

If you asked yourself what education was for, what would your answer be? Many people might say that its purpose was to develop a well-rounded child, to enable children to get on well with others, to be curious about the world, and to have a positive self-image. However, it is easy to forget the importance of these things if there is an over-emphasis on passing examinations and boosting school league table positions. Clearly, it is essential that children reach their own potential, but cooperation is a more useful life skill than competition in developing Global Citizens.

Young people are our future, but they are also our present. They are interested and concerned about what is happening in the world, and in their lifetimes could make a difference to the inherited problems they face. However, we cannot leave it to our children to sort out all the difficulties. As adults – teachers and educationalists – we can take the responsibility to begin the process of change. We can provide an education that will furnish children with the knowledge, skills and attitudes that will enable them to see that the issues of the world are issues for them. Such an education is in line with current government thinking, and is exciting and relevant for young people. It is important not to lose sight of this in the face of overwhelming demands on the curriculum.

Global Citizenship must be at the heart of education. This is because it is good education, as well as for all of the following reasons.

The world we live in is unfair and unequal, and Global Citizenship promotes the challenging and changing of this.

There is injustice and poverty within and between societies. In Britain, poverty has been cited as a cause of underachievement at school, as well as physical, emotional and social damage (*Guardian,* 14 Sept, 1999). Globally, there are many shocking statistics to illustrate inequality.

The 1998 *Human Development Report* from the UN stated that the amount people in Europe and North America spend a year on pet food, cosmetics and perfume ($37 billion) would provide basic education, water and sanitation, basic health and nutrition to all those without those things, with $9bn left over (UNDP, 1998).

We live in a diverse society, and Global Citizenship gives children the tools to counter ignorance and intolerance within it.

Ignorance and intolerance take many forms. Attitudes of empathy and respect for diversity, as well as skills of cooperation and negotiation, are essential to combat the prejudice and discrimination currently alive and kicking in our society.

Global Citizenship enables the challenging of misinformation and stereotyped views that exist about Majority World countries.

There are many generalisations, assumptions and half-truths in the public domain, especially, although not exclusively, about Majority World countries. Unbiased learning requires critical thinking – a key element of Global Citizenship.

Global Citizenship is exciting and relevant to children.

An unpublished survey by Oxfam Education showed that the majority of primary-school children approached had an interest in and awareness of local and global issues. The children gave some very practical ideas as to how they could change things in the future, for example:

- walk instead of going in the car
- lobby the council for local changes
- buy more things in charity shops
- try to think what it would be like if you didn't have enough to eat
- be more friendly to others at school
- watch the news so you know what is going on in the world.

We live in an interdependent world, and Global Citizenship encourages us to recognise our responsibilities towards each other.

There are many similarities and links between people across the globe, not only in terms of personal needs and aspirations, but also regarding communications and trade. How far can you send an e-mail? Where have the tasty items in your kitchen cupboards come from?

We live in a rapidly changing world and Global Citizenship is about flexibility and adaptability as well as about a positive image of the future.

If children are to hope for a fairer and safer future, they need a clear vision of what this would look like, as well as the means to attain it. As Professor Patricia J. Williams, of Columbia University said, when she gave the 1997 Radio 4 Reith Lectures on 'The Paradox of Race' (1997: 14):

> I do think that to a very great extent we dream our worlds into being … an optimistic course might be charted, if only we could imagine it.

Global Citizenship acknowledges that we have power as individuals: each of us can change things, and each of us has choices about how we behave.

We can:

- speak up against injustice and discrimination
- bank with an ethical investor
- reduce waste – refuse unnecessary packaging, reuse and recycle as much as possible
- buy Fair Trade products
- become activists – take encouragement from the genetically modified (GM) foods debate: the Iceland supermarket chain banned GM foods after investigations prompted by six letters from a church group in Blackburn.

Central to Global Citizenship is the importance of learning from the experience of others, both in our own society and beyond it.

There are numerous examples of Global Citizenship in the UK and all over the world. A whole village in Orissa, India, became involved in a Sustainable Development initiative, described in *Thengapalli* (see Chapter 6). This is a notice from the headquarters of the initiative (Hampshire CC Education 1997) that might inspire us all!

> What you spend years building may be destroyed overnight.
> *Build anyway.*
>
> Give the world the best you have and you will get kicked.
> *Give the world the best you have anyway.*
>
> The biggest people with the biggest ideas can be shot down by the smallest people with the smallest minds.
> *Think big anyway.*
>
> If you do good, people will accuse you of selfish, ulterior motives.
> *Do good anyway.*

Teaching approaches used to promote Global Citizenship have a positive impact on pupils and can raise standards.

Four aspects of this are as follows.

1. The principles, ideas and activities in this Handbook cover much of the inspection criteria for primary schools, especially in the areas of quality of education, raising educational standards and pupils' values, attitudes and personal development.
2. Research by Stephen Scoffham (1999) suggests that children's attitudes about Majority World countries can be affected in a positive way through education.
3. Active teaching methods such as enquiries, drama and simulations are particularly successful in promoting learning (Fisher and Hicks, 1987).
4. Research by Lynn Davies at Birmingham University (1999) showed that the involvement of pupils in decision-making systems, such as in school councils, could lead to a drop in exclusion levels where the school ethos supports democracy and equity and values both pupil and teacher performance and welfare.

Finally ... addressing concerns

Many teachers we have worked with support the principles of Global Citizenship, and feel that these should form the core of education. Indeed, this Handbook contains many suggestions from educators for including Global Citizenship in schools. However, there may be some teachers who have concerns about how, when and where these principles can be incorporated into their everyday practice. The following table illustrates this. The left-hand column is an amalgamation of responses from primary teachers when asked about the difficulties they might face when trying to implement Global Citizenship in schools. The right-hand column shows how we will try to address these concerns in this Handbook.

Teacher concerns	Support offered
■ How can we implement a whole-school approach?	■ Some ideas are given in Chapter 2.
■ How can we gain clarity and shared views as to what constitutes Global Citizenship?	■ Explore the ideas and activities suggested in Chapter 2. These include a series of in-service sessions, which can either be run during staff meetings or as half-day or whole-day events.
■ How can I integrate Global Citizenship into the curriculum?	■ This Handbook shows how Global Citizenship can be integrated into schools through activities, ideas and slight adjustments to existing practice.
■ I don't have time to pack any more into the curriculum!	■ Global Citizenship is not another subject area for you to take on: it is a way of teaching. If you look at the matrices on pages 53–56, you will probably see that you are already covering many of its principles.
■ Aren't some of the issues quite complex for children to understand?	■ Many global issues have parallels with classroom ones, for example the need to share the world's resources as well as to share classroom games (see Chapter 2, worksheet 1, page 16 for activity). Fairness is something we all, especially children, can relate to.
■ How can I find out more about issues of Global Citizenship?	■ Chapter 6 gives resources and contacts for background information about issues of Global Citizenship, some for you and some for children.
■ Will parents like the idea of Global Citizenship?	■ If parents understand Global Citizenship and its benefits for their children and themselves, they are likely to support it. See Chapter 2, page 35 for suggestions as to how to involve them closely with all aspects of school life; for example, hold a Global Citizenship Open Day, invite parents to help at school, work with them on community projects, hold an in-service session for them.
■ How can I provide an all-round picture of a country or an issue, and avoid perpetuating stereotypes?	■ See Chapter 2, Activity 3, page 20, for a way to address this.
■ How can I ensure that 'appreciating diversity' doesn't lead to tokenism, and that it really leads to effective tackling of racist behaviour?	■ Increase your own knowledge of the issues – using this Handbook should help you do that, as will the contacts and resources in Chapter 6. Find other support by discussing issues within the school and with neighbouring schools, and by inviting an 'expert' to lead an in-service session.
■ How can I make Global Citizenship 'real' in predominantly mono-cultural areas?	■ Do the activities in Chapter 3. Global Citizenship is relevant in all areas, not only those of high ethnic diversity. It is about fairness and equity for all: issues of Global Citizenship are just as important in the Cornish fishing village of Mousehole as they are in the city of Glasgow.

References

Annan, Kofi, 'Why Make a Special Case for Children?' **www.unicef.org/crc/specialcase** 14/05/01

Davies, Lynn (1999) *Schools Councils and Pupil Exclusions*, Schools Council UK.

Davies, Nick 'Poverty is the key – not just an excuse', *The Guardian*, 14 Sept 1999.

Developing a global dimension in the school curriculum (2000) (produced by DfEE, DfID, QCA, the Development Education Association and Central Bureau)

Fisher, S. and Hicks, D. (1987) *World Studies, 8–13*, Oliver and Boyd.

Oxfam (1997) *A Curriculum for Global Citizenship*.

Scoffham, Stephen (1999) 'Young Children's Perception of the World' in *Teaching Young Children*, Tricia David (ed.), Paul Chapman Publishing.

The Global Dimension in the Curriculum (2001) Learning and Teaching Scotland in collaboration with DfID, Scottish Executive, and IDEAS.

The Stephen Lawrence Inquiry: Report of an inquiry by Sir William MacPherson of Cluny (The MacPherson Report) (1999) The Stationery Office.

Theodore, Dylan (1997) *Thengapalli*, Hampshire CC/Hampshire DEC.

United Nations Development Programme (UNDP) (1998) *Human Development Report*, New York: OUP.

Williams, Patricia J. (1997) *Seeing a Colour-blind Future: The Paradox of Race*, Virago Press.

Chapter 2
Global Citizenship in the whole school

This chapter looks at the implementation of Global Citizenship across the whole school. It looks at the contribution of teaching and non-teaching staff, governors/school board members, and parents. The use of the word 'educator' in this chapter reflects this, since Global Citizenship is relevant to everyone involved in educating or supporting pupils within or outside the classroom.

There are two elements to this chapter:

1 developing understanding and exploring the issues of Global Citizenship; this section provides some in-service (INSET) ideas for whole-school work
2 guidance on doing a whole-school Global Citizenship audit, with examples of good practice for your inspiration.

Developing understanding of Global Citizenship: whole-school in-service activities

The easiest way to become an educator who promotes Global Citizenship is if you are supported by your colleagues and the wider school community through a whole-school approach. This approach requires that pupils, teaching and non-teaching staff, governors and school boards, and parents agree on and implement basic principles. For example, a school's policy on diversity should be reflected in classroom work and corridor displays and reinforced by supervisors in the dinner hall, as well as by parents in the community. The purpose is to be inclusive: if everyone feels involved in the school, and in agreement with the school's aims, it is more likely that the aims will be achieved.

A whole-school approach can be promoted through initial teacher education and all of the following:

- in-service training
- school policies
- the school's ethos, as demonstrated in displays and resources, as well as in everyday practice within and outside the classroom
- meetings with all those constituting the whole school
- interaction with the local community beyond that immediately included in the whole school.

Global Citizenship: The Handbook for Primary Teaching

The following in-service activities each illustrate different aspects of Global Citizenship, and can be used individually or as a series of training sessions as a starting point for the development of a whole-school Global Citizenship approach. Individual sessions are designed to be part of whole-school staff meetings. Each session will take between 45 and 60 minutes. Another option would be to run an in-service day covering several of the activities. Activities 1 and 2 will need two sessions to complete – these are shown as Part A and Part B. Activities 3, 4 and 5 cover different ways of presenting positive images.

The way in which the activities are undertaken is important. The sessions should promote discussion and creative thinking, allow for the weighing-up of all reasoned opinions, and enable participants to learn from each other. Although suggestions are made and guidance given, the outcomes of sessions will depend on the process and on the participants.

Theme *What is a Global Citizen?*

Activity 1

Aim — **For participants to think about what they understand a 'Global Citizen' to be, and to look at how this could translate into educational practice.**

Part A

1. Working in small groups, ask participants to come up with ideas about what traits or characteristics a Global Citizen would have. These should be written on post-it notes – one idea on each.

2. Give out an A3 copy of the diagram 'Traits for the educator aspiring to be a Global Citizen' to each group. Ask participants to stick their post-its on the A3 sheet to correspond broadly with the nine traits. Centre discussion in each group on questions such as:
   - How similar are the participants' ideas and the diagram?
   - How helpful are the traits in furthering understanding of what a Global Citizen might be? (Encourage participants to read through the diagram either individually or as a group and place themselves on a scale from 'yes', through 'getting there' to 'no'.)
   - Do any unmatched post-its represent completely new traits which should be included?

3. In a plenary session share feedback from each group.

Note: *Keep the papers for Part B.*

Figure 2: Traits for the educator aspiring to be a Global Citizen

In addition to having a sense of humour and fun, a Global Citizen who is an educator:

feels empathy with others
- listens carefully to what pupils have to say and values their contribution and experiences
- promotes an understanding that throughout the world people have common needs and rights
- is compassionate and sensitive towards others
- tries to see the world through the eyes of others

has an understanding of and active commitment to sustainable development
- is concerned about the amount of the world's resources that are being used daily and finds ways of using less
- shows respect and concern for the environment and all life within it
- considers the needs of future generations in relation to their present lifestyle
- encourages pupils to think creatively about their own vision for the future, and how it can be achieved

has a sense of identity and self-esteem, and promotes these feelings in others
- recognises the value of individuality in oneself and others
- acknowledges that we all make mistakes and that we can learn from them
- has high and achievable expectations of all pupils, and tries to ensure that each pupil fulfils their own potential
- praises pupils and creates an inclusive, secure and nurturing environment for them

has an understanding of peace and conflict, and has the ability and willingness to behave cooperatively and resolve conflict
- encourages children to cooperate, share, take turns, and take responsibility for their actions
- ensures that there is a democratic class system in place where pupils can share their problems and where grievances can be resolved, such as 'circle time'
- has a clear and fair procedure for pupils and educator to follow if conflict erupts

has an understanding of and active commitment to, social justice and equity
- is aware of causes of inequality in the world, deeply concerned by its injustices, and committed to changing things
- is aware of the educator's own rights and responsibilities, and respectful of the rights of others
- behaves democratically within and outside school
- uses fairness as the basis for decision-making

has the ability to think critically, challenge injustice and argue effectively
- is aware of their own opinions, but able and willing to challenge and change them in the light of convincing evidence
- is able to present an informed, persuasive argument based on reason
- does not generalise about peoples, countries, continents
- is able to recognise and challenge bias and manipulation of information in books, ICT and the media

has an understanding of and respect for diversity
- treats pupils as different but equal
- enables all children to have equal access to education, whatever their needs
- is aware of issues related to diversity of race, gender, disability, religion and sexual orientation and is sensitive to the challenges faced by those who may be seen as 'different'
- is actively anti-discriminatory

has an understanding of globalisation and interdependence, and an active commitment to learning more about such issues
- is curious about the world and committed to lifelong learning in order to understand how it works in a variety of ways
- has a range of resources available in the classroom which enable pupils to gain information about the world and its issues
- recognises that global issues are complex
- realises that many areas of Global Citizenship have the potential to be contentious, but that this does not reduce the need to address them

has a belief that people can make a difference
- has the confidence to act in order to improve situations
- is an active participant in their school and community and sees the two as interlinked
- promotes active learning

Part B

1. Working in the same groups as for the first activity, ask each group to cut up their A3 paper from last time so that each of the nine original traits, and any additional ones, are on separate pieces of paper. Ask each group to discuss the relative importance of each trait, and to arrange them in an order that reflects this. It is important to make clear that there is no 'correct' formation.

2. After about 15 minutes, encourage the participants to walk around the room and look at how other groups have arranged their pieces of paper.

3. In a plenary session, allow each group to state which traits they felt were most important and why. Also encourage reflection on the process of the exercise: did each group member feel his or her views were incorporated into the final formation? If not, why?

4. Look at each trait and discuss which of them the school already has, and which should be strengthened. Record this on a chart under the headings:

    (a) Already being done

    (b) Should be done right away

    (c) Should be done in the long term

    (d) Would be difficult to do given the present situation.

5. Finally, back in groups, ask each group to choose one point written under (b) or (c) on the chart and to consider how it could be achieved within the school. (It may be helpful to refer to the second part of this chapter for good practice ideas.) Ask each group to record their thoughts on large sheets of paper, so that they may be displayed around the room for informal sharing. These ideas could contribute to the developing of a whole-school audit.

Theme 'Contentious' issues

Dealing with some of the issues related to Global Citizenship, such as poverty, the effects of globalisation, and human rights, might present educators with some difficulties. Such issues may also seem contentious, although each of us will have our own view about this. Bringing global issues to a local (personal or classroom) level and working on possible solutions to problems is one starting point.

Activity 2

Aim **To show that there are parallels between global and local issues and for educators to address 'contentious' issues.**

Part A

(This exercise is adapted from Brownlie (1995:13).)

This activity could also be done with pupils, in which case try to de-personalise issues as far as possible, and allow time for pupils to talk about things individually with you if they wish.

1. Give one A4 copy of the tables 'Global issues and 'Classroom issues' (Worksheet 1) to each group of participants.
2. As a whole group, discuss the lists to ensure participants' understanding of each term.
3. In groups, ask the participants to link the global and classroom issues. (Note that the order of the entries under each heading is not intentionally matched, and each issue has more than one link.)
4. Ask participants to note some real examples of each of the classroom issues.
5. Ask them to decide on one issue which they feel would present them with particular difficulties in the classroom. Together, formulate possible strategies for dealing with this situation.
6. Share these strategies with the whole group, and discuss whether existing school policies and practice incorporate them already, or should incorporate them.
7. End the session by reflecting on the *Dear Teacher* letter (Steiner 1993:12) (Worksheet 2).

Worksheet 1

Global issues	Classroom issues
Environmental awareness	Name calling
Peace and conflict	Arguing over things
Justice	Excluding others
Interdependence	Complaining that things aren't fair
Discrimination	Wasting things
Distribution of resources	Sharing
Prejudice	Fighting
Choice and action	Deciding what to do

Worksheet 2

Dear Teacher

I am a survivor of a concentration camp. My eyes saw what no man should witness: gas chambers built by learned engineers; children poisoned by educated physicians; infants killed by trained nurses; women and babies shot by high-school and college graduates.

So I am suspicious of education.

My request is: help your students to become more human. Your efforts must never produce learned monsters, skilled psychopaths, educated Eichmanns.

Reading, writing and arithmetic are important only if they serve to make our children more human.

Activity 2

Part B

1. Give out a copy of the 'Discussion prompts' (Worksheet 3) and ask participants to jot down the implications of some or all of these statements for their work in school.
2. In a feedback session, ask one group to lead on each issue, and then open up for wider discussion.

Worksheet 3

Discussion prompts

1 Many problems such as wars and famine may be complex and difficult for children as well as adults to understand. However, children often experience the basic concepts behind such issues. Both in and out of school, children are often encouraged to play with others without fighting, to share things, and to take turns. They will also feel that some things are fair or unfair, and will meet kindness as well as unkindness.

2 In some cases, the children in our classrooms have themselves been subject to human rights violations: they may be refugees, they may have witnessed violent scenes, and they may have been abused. To avoid 'contentious issues', or to pretend they do not occur, or to regard them as unsuitable for particular age groups, is to deny the real lives of some children.

3 To avoid addressing racism is tantamount to supporting it. As suggested by the teacher educator Russell Jones (1999:161), the negative experiences of schooling gained by many black children in our society are 'the consequence of silence'.

4 Teaching children to think about controversial issues is important in the development of critical thinking skills. Children need to be able to weigh up different viewpoints and distinguish between fact and opinion if they are to hold reasoned views.

Theme *Presenting positive images in work with people, places and artefacts*

Activity 3

Aim	**To help educators develop ideas on how to promote positive images of people, places and artefacts. The 'do' and 'don't' lists in this activity are central to all aspects of Global Citizenship.**

1 Start with this exercise, which can be done briefly. Show the participants two photographs illustrating different aspects of the same place, for example: the front entrance of the school and where the dustbins are kept; the smartest house in the town and the worst eyesore. Alternatively, make all participants a small paper frame. Take them outside and ask them to look at a view through their frame, and then turn 180 degrees and look again. What do the different views show? Discuss what impression each view makes of the place – points about the dangers of generalising and the need for an all-round picture will probably be made.

2 Asking participants to bear this activity in mind, give out a copy of the 'Do and Don't' table (Worksheet 4) to each group.

3 Ask participants to choose one point, from either column, and come up with an idea as to how it could practically be achieved within the whole school – either through school ethos, displays, or an assembly or class activity.

4 Share this in a plenary session, and incorporate ideas into school policy or a whole-school Global Citizenship audit.

It is important to consider the two lists in all work about people, places or artefacts.

Worksheet 4

Do	Don't
Give an all-round picture of any place, country or people you are presenting to pupils by showing pictures of both townscapes and rural areas, the modern and the traditional, rich and poor, youth and old people. Show people engaging in leisure pursuits as well as work. There is enjoyment and contentment everywhere, as well as problems and difficulties.	Generalise about peoples, countries and continents. It is impossible to describe 'an African house', just as it is 'a European house'. There is infinite variety in both continents.
Treat photographs of people and artefacts sensitively. Perhaps imagine that the person in the picture, or the person who made the artefact, is in the room. Be clear about your purpose in asking pupils to undertake particular activities: what are you hoping the pupils will gain? How will the work promote the appreciation of diversity? How will it challenge stereotypes?	Make assumptions about people and places in photographs, or about artefacts. Instead try to find out as much as possible about them, and be cautious about things you say.
Ensure like is compared to like if asking children to make comparisons. For instance, a clay pot from rural Malawi, designed to keep water cool cannot fairly be compared with an expensively produced Royal Doulton vase made for decoration. Similarly, rural Wales cannot be meaningfully compared with Kathmandu. In looking for similarities and differences between places, peoples and lifestyles, first look for the commonalities such as basic human needs, for example shelter, food, water and transport. Focus on common aspirations. Often differences in, for instance, housing, food or transport are the result of what is appropriate for a particular situation or what is available locally.	Think of certain cultures as being 'exotic' or 'primitive' – this could lead to misguided feelings of superiority among pupils. Encourage positive images of all cultures and countries. All civilisations that have lived on earth have made particular contributions to the development of the world – some negative, some positive.
Consider context in trying to understand an artefact: its cultural background, the place and time it is from and the purpose behind its creation. Context is also significant for photographs. Why, where and when was the photograph taken? Who is the person pictured? What do we know about them? Do you think they gave permission for the photograph to be taken? What was the photographer's purpose?	Be patronising about people, places or artefacts.
Recognise appropriate technology as good technology – the use of readily available materials and tools is sensible, sustainable and practical. Encourage recognition and respect for ways of doing things which are different from those familiar to pupils.	Encourage unfair comparisons.

Theme *Presenting positive images through using artefacts*

Artefacts are interesting and enjoyable to work with, and can help to bring cultures alive. They stimulate pupils' curiosity, discussion, creativity and powers of observation and detection. They help pupils realise the limits of their understanding, as well as encouraging their research skills in finding out more.

Handling artefacts can develop pupils' ability to respect and care for things sensitively – necessary because they are part of people's everyday lives. As Rigoberta Menchu Tum, the Guatemalan activist, pointed out (in Burr 1991: 25):

> What hurts us most is that our costumes are considered beautiful, but it is as if the person wearing them didn't exist.

Artefacts can be acquired from a number of sources: charity shops, from Fair Trade catalogues, markets, or from collecting them (or asking others to do so) when visiting different places. Here are some suggestions of the kinds of artefacts that may be useful in building up a collection from one particular country – in this case Tanzania:

- a stove
- a coconut grater
- a radio
- a stamp
- a crisp packet
- a toy made from recycled wire
- a musical instrument
- a *kanga* – a multi-purpose piece of material used, for instance, for carrying children and wearing as a wrap (some have Kiswahili writing on them, which would be of added interest)
- some locally produced coffee
- a training shoe
- a sisal bag or basket.

Such a range of items may enable pupils to realise that some things are common to many countries, to appreciate the ingenuity of Tanzanian craftspeople, and to see that there are various ways of doing things.

Activity 4

Aim — **To help educators develop ideas on how to promote positive images of artefacts, people and places, through work with artefacts.**

1 Ask participants in small groups to list five artefacts that represent the country they are in.

2 Share with the whole group, giving reasons for choosing each item. Discuss what impression of the country would be given by this representation.

3 Then choose one of the artefacts and apply the following list of questions to it. These constitute some points to think about before starting work with artefacts.

- What aspect of life does this artefact portray?
- What else would you include to give an all-round view of a place or country?
- What do you know about the artefact?

- What would you like to know about it? (If you do not know much about an artefact you want to use, do not be afraid to tell pupils so – the processes of questioning and of finding out are both valuable. There are many ways of finding out – books, the internet, asking others.)
- What sort of comments do you predict others might make about it? Think about your reasons.
- What sort of comments do you want others to make about it? Think about your reasons.

Incidentally, these questions can be applied to any artefacts, and would be a good starting point for pupils' work in the classroom.

4   Then encourage participants to focus on the last two questions and brainstorm ideas on:
- ways of dealing with negative comments that might arise from work with artefacts
- what questions to ask about artefacts which will be likely to prompt positive responses.

5   Amalgamate everyone's ideas to produce a useful reference list for each of the two areas above in future work:
- ideas for strategies to combat prejudice
- good questions to ask when using artefacts.

Theme *Presenting positive images through promoting critical thinking: 'Bias Alert!' – a look at multimedia resources*

Activity 5

Aim **To develop the ability to think, listen and read critically.**

This idea is adapted from *Issues in Race and Education* no. 44, Spring 1985, published by the Association of London Teachers Against Racism and Fascism (ALTARF). Called 'Book Look', it is still useful in classrooms today. The original idea was to have a slip of paper to put into any book that pupils felt was racist or sexist. For Global Citizenship purposes we have re-named it 'Bias Alert!' and added notes on other forms of bias. To modernise the activity, we have made the form appropriate for assessing any paper or electronic resource.

1   Give out a selection of resources to each group (book, CD-ROM, newspaper cutting) and/or enable access to a website. To enable pupils to practice looking for bias ensure that some resources contain clear examples.

2   Give out a Bias Alert! form (Worksheet 5) and the notes on different biases (Worksheet 6) to each group of participants.

3   Ask the group to look at the resources, and complete their form giving reasons for concern – these comments are a warning to others (who may or may not agree).

4   Discuss the findings as a whole group, and decide whether the idea would be useful in the school, either as it is presented here or in modified form.

Note: *Although we have suggested this as an in-service session, it is really intended for pupils to do. If your school decides to introduce such a scheme, futher work with pupils on critical reading and bias detection would be necessary beforehand. (See Chapter 3.)*

Worksheet 5

Bias Alert!

Type of resource ....

Author ....

Title..

Date of publication..

I think this resource is:

racist/sexist/unfair to the disabled/unfair to those with less 'traditional' family relationships/outdated*

because of its:

language ....(page/location) ....

pictures ....(page/location) ....

story ....(page/location) ....

other reason ....(page/location) ....

Any further comments..

....

....

I think this resource should be:

kept with a Bias Alert! sticker on it/put in the recycling bin*

Name ....

Class...

Date ....

*delete as appropriate.

Worksheet 6

Notes on different biases

You or the pupils may wish to add to the points listed in these notes.

Three questions which apply to all the biases in the 'Bias Alert!' form

1 Are issues tackled honestly?

2 What are the hidden messages?

3 Is there a diverse and balanced presentation of society?

Race

How are black people portrayed – as individuals speaking for themselves or groups, as having a variety of attributes, both personal characteristics and lifestyle, or in a tokenistic way? From whose viewpoint is the resource written? Are generalisations made? Are black people left out? Are the illustrations convincing? Are pejorative or racist terms used? ('black' is used politically here.)

(Adapted from Epstein and Sealey, 1990)

Disability

How are disabled people portrayed? As professional people going about their everyday lives, and able to make a significant contribution to society, or as needing help?

Gender issues

Who is doing what? Are women shown only in 'traditional' roles of wife or mother? Are they shown as being passive rather than as 'doers'; as without responsible jobs or power, with men being the ones in charge? Are generalisations made about men – for example, are they all depicted as unemotional, or liking lager and football? Are both sexes represented in books among the examples of influential figures in history, writers, scientists, and opinion-formers?

Relationships

How are family relationships and family groups portrayed? Is a diverse range of families shown, including lone-parent families or same-sex relationships?

Theme *Sustainable development*

Activity 6

Aim   For participants to think about what sustainable development means in relation to their own lifestyles as well as to the school and community.

1. Give each group of participants the three quotations provided (Worksheet 7), and ask them which one they feel best describes sustainable development, and why. (There is no 'right' answer!) Ask them to arrange the statements to show their order of preference. If the group does not agree on the order, arrange the statements to reflect this – perhaps in a line.

2. Invite the participants to walk around the room to look at how other groups have arranged their statements.

3. Then give out to participants the statement on sustainable development from Cardiff County Council and the seven key concepts of sustainable development identified by the Panel for Education for Sustainable Development (1999) (Worksheet 8). Ask participants to discuss how these definitions relate to their earlier views of sustainable development.

4. Give participants a chance to share their thoughts as a whole.

5. Then separate the groups into two halves. Ask half of the groups to design the layout, policies and practices of a school that is a model for the promotion of sustainable development. Ask the other half to do the same but for a school that is against the promotion of sustainable development. The table below may help with some ideas on ways of promoting healthy sustainable lifestyles at school. The list of ideas is far from exhaustive.

6. Share ideas in a plenary session, possibly including discussion about which model your school most resembles.

How can we help ourselves to be healthy?	*look after our bodies*	*avoid harmful substances*	*travel to and from school safely*	*move round the school safely*	*protect ourselves from the sun*
How can the school help us?	■ encourage us to eat healthy food: sell fruit and vegetables in a playtime tuck-shop ■ teach us to look after our bodies, as well as about the dangers of smoking, HIV/AIDS, excessive drinking, etc. ■ ensure that there is a pleasant and safe school environment	■ use biodegradable and non-toxic cleaning fluids ■ remind us that medicines can be harmful	■ remind us about road safety ■ implement a walk-to-school initiative ■ remind us not to go with strangers	■ minimise barriers to moving safely, e.g. steep steps, no handrail, uneven paving ■ ensure that pupils move around the school in a considerate way	■ have a shady and quiet playground area

Note: *You could adapt this table for use with children. Present blank or partially completed grids for completion. See what they come up with – and whether and how their ideas could be accommodated.*

Worksheet 7

Quotations about sustainable development

Quotation 1

❝ *The Earth provides enough to satisfy everyone's needs, but not for everyone's greed.* ❞

Mahatma Gandhi, www.ieer.org/latest/oct2quote.html

Quotation 2

❝ *The Earth belongs to everyone, not part of it to certain people but all of it to everyone, to be enjoyed and cared for.* ❞

Michael Foreman, *Dinosaurs and all that Rubbish* (1999)

Quotation 3

❝ *The interconnectedness of life is both a blessing and a curse; possibilities are boundless and consequences endless. Every value judgement we make ripples into a life somewhere.* ❞

Paula Owens, Deputy Head, Eastchurch Primary School, Kent (2001)

Worksheet 8

Local and global sustainability

> *Our collective activities and behaviour contribute to international problems such as global warming, climate change and deforestation. Our local actions, for example in what we buy, can have positive and negative consequences for communities living elsewhere in the world where these goods are produced.*

Cardiff County Council, *Local Sustainability Strategy for Cardiff*, 2000

Seven key concepts of sustainable development (Panel for Education for Sustainable Development, 1999)

1 Interdependence
Understanding how people, the environment and the economy are inextricably linked at all levels from local to global.

2 Citizenship and stewardship
Recognising the importance of taking individual responsibility and action to ensure the world is a better place.

3 Needs and rights of future generations
Understanding our own basic needs and the implications for the needs of future generations of actions taken today.

4 Diversity
Respecting and valuing both human diversity (cultural, social and economic) and biodiversity.

5 Quality of life
Acknowledging that global equity and justice are essential elements of sustainability and that basic needs must be met universally.

6 Sustainable change
Understanding that resources are finite and that this has implications for people's lifestyles and for commerce and industry.

7 Balance
Understanding of uncertainty and of the need for precautions in action.

Theme *Linking with the community – welcoming visitors*

Invited visitors can cause great excitement and offer huge benefits to pupils and staff alike, especially if both you and the visitor are well prepared beforehand. This activity aims to generate discussion about what to consider when inviting visitors into school and what visitors might find helpful for their own preparation. Here are a few points which you might like to throw into the discussion when participants are making lists of suggestions for a successful visit.

- Is the visitor aware of and in agreement with the school's aims and ethos, the policies on Equal Opportunities, and codes of behaviour?
- Are they clear about the pupils' and your own expectations, and the level at which to pitch the presentation?
- Are you clear about and happy with what the visitor intends to do?
- Are you and the visitor sure about the pronunciation of each other's names?
- Are you clear about how the visitor wishes to be introduced?

Activity 7

1. In groups, ask the participants to choose a classroom topic, and then suggest visitors who might be helpful in its teaching.

2. Next ask them to focus on one of their suggested visitors, and make two lists. First, everything the visitor would need to know before their visit. Second, everything you as hosts would need to have considered in order to make the visit successful. (Refer to the ideas above if necessary.)

3. In a plenary session, amalgamate the views from the groups. Aim to produce some practical and agreed 'Guidelines for Visits' – some relating to the school, others to the visitor. To maximise the mutual benefit to visitor and school, the Guidelines should be available for staff reference, and those applicable to visitors should be sent out before the visit.

4. To end the session, distribute copies of the 'Visitor checklist' (Worksheet 9) from Sanders and Swinden (1990) and discuss with the person next to you. This is particularly useful in ensuring that pupils maximise the experience of preparing for and looking after a visitor. It relates to both the process and content of a visit.

Note: *Suggestions of organisations able to go into schools are in Chapter 6.*

Worksheet 9

Visitor checklist

Our visitor is ....

We shall meet him/her at................................... (time/place).

S/he will be staying for .... minutes.

We shall offer refreshments in .... (place).

My suggested plan of the room for the visit is

....

....

....

Who will do what? (This might involve more than one person.)

.... will collect the visitor.

.... will offer refreshments.

.... will introduce the visitor.

.... will keep time.

.... will take notes.

.... will ask the first question.

.... will close the visit.

.... will ask the visitor if there is anything else he or she wants to say.

.... will ask how the visitor is feeling.

.... will thank the visitor.

.... will take the visitor out.

Can you think of any other jobs to be done?

....

....

....

Global Citizenship: The Handbook for Primary Teaching © Chris Kington Publishing and Oxfam GB 2002

One way to develop all of the ideas generated through these in-service activities into school policy and practice is to devise a whole-school Global Citizenship audit.

Whole-school audit

The table 'Whole-school Global Citizenship audit' (Worksheet 10) gives a possible outline of an audit. It sets out key areas for consideration in the devising of a whole-school Global Citizenship approach. It can be adapted to suit your own educational circumstances, so you may want to add your own points. The columns can be enlarged and the first four used to record your starting position. The last column, 'Action points', could contain ideas of how progress could be made along a Global Citizenship path. It is important that these action points are achievable, and widely endorsed, because for change to be successful and sustained it is important that everyone works together.

The order of the points is not significant.

Worksheet 10

Whole-school Global Citizenship audit

As a school we have...	Excellent	OK	Working Towards	Evidence	Action Points
1 Global Citizenship as part of the school's mission statement, and included in all curriculum planning					
2 A welcoming, safe and nurturing school environment, where the self-esteem of pupils and adults is reaffirmed					
3 An effective Equal Opportunities policy					
4 An effective behaviour management policy including clear display of what these policies are in the school					
5 A commitment to democratic and inclusive processes, including an effective Schools Council					
6 A variety of teaching methods to engage pupils and support and increase their motivation to effect change					
7 Whole-school initiatives and events to promote aspects of Global Citizenship					
8 An open, effective and inclusive governing body/school board with representation to reflect the full diversity of the school and community					
9 Purchasing and banking practices which promote Global Citizenship					
10 A commitment to learn from the experiences of people from diverse backgrounds and from around the world					
11 A commitment to sustainable development, e.g. a policy for recycling, waste reduction and energy saving					
12 Resources and displays which celebrate diversity, and include positive examples of different cultures, genders, disabilities, and types of family group					
13 Active links between the school, parents and the wider community					
14 Support for staff wishing to increase their own knowledge and understanding of Global Citizenship					

Global Citizenship: The Handbook for Primary Teaching   © Chris Kington Publishing and Oxfam GB 2002

Examples of good practice in Global Citizenship

The following ideas give support and suggestions for developing action points and expanding on the areas outlined in the whole-school Global Citizenship audit.

Mission statement

- Wendy Horden, Head at St Mary's CE (Aided) Primary School in Staffordshire adapted the school's mission statement to reflect Global Citizenship. It now includes:

  > We aim to produce understanding citizens of the twenty first century who recognise the need to participate in a caring and responsible way for the sustainability of our world.

- Ensure the mission statement is part of the school development plan so that it is ongoing and reviewed.

Providing a supportive environment and raising self-esteem

- Make space and time to listen to and talk to children about their interests and concerns.
- There are many activities in Chapter 3 for raising pupils' self-esteem.
- Some good ideas for raising the self-esteem of staff can be found in Mosley (1993). For instance:
  - *for staff meetings*: use different rooms around the school – teachers formally inviting others to their room; have some meetings outside school, perhaps where good teas are served; ensure that non-teaching staff are at all meetings and draw up and stick to a set of 'golden rules'.
  - *in the staff room*: agree basic ground rules – for example, talk to staff who may feel isolated, avoid using 'put-downs', avoid forming cliques, and make more effort to praise and support each other; set up a staff room committee; have a buffet lunch every fortnight for all staff, and coffee and cake for all staff on Fridays.

Effective Equal Opportunities policy

- Look at the school's Equal Opportunities policy and how it works in practice. This ranges from whole-school, shared procedures for effectively tackling racism and bullying to ensuring Equal Opportunities works for disabled parents, visitors, and governors and school board members. This includes easy access, appropriate toilets and induction loops in the Hall to facilitate hearing. If there are no disabled pupils in the school, discuss what factors prevent this, and how they could be addressed to make the school more inclusive.
- Dadzie (2000) suggests ideas to improve a school's anti-racist ethos. These include having an unambiguous anti-racist message conveyed throughout the school; ensuring that there are black and ethnic minority parents involved where possible in all aspects of the school's work and decision making; ensuring access to professional interpreters; and providing lunches which reflect the range of pupils' tastes and requirements.
- Staff at Southwell Primary School in Dorset carried out a risk assessment of the school in preparation for the arrival of a new blind pupil. They invited a teacher for the visually impaired from the LEA to run a session to raise their own awareness of practical issues. Then pupils, inmates from the local prison, and members of the community joined together to raise funds and make an adventure trail in the school grounds for the new pupil.

Behaviour management

- There are many examples of anti-bullying and peer mediation initiatives in schools. For example: Year 6 pupils at Bishop Monkton C of E School, North Yorkshire, wear yellow caps at playtime to advertise that they are on hand to deal with problems other pupils may face.
- Pupils at Gray's Infants School, East Sussex, earn 'gold cards' for coming into assembly quietly and sensibly. At the end of the week the class with the most cards has five minutes extra play time.
- The Development Education Centre in South Yorkshire has facilitated links between a peer mediation project operating in schools in northern Ghana and schemes in schools in Sheffield. Pupils share their experiences and understanding of conflict and its resolution on personal, societal and global levels.
- Many of the activities in Chapter 3 promote behaviour management strategies.

Democratic and inclusive processes

- Many schools have effective Schools Councils with real responsibilities. The Schools Council UK (1998), state that a school or classroom council can enable pupils to develop their skills in:

> ... presenting reasoned arguments; listening and responding calmly to points of view that are critical of their own; contributing towards problem-solving on issues of mutual concern; working effectively with others to create social harmony within the class; learning peer mediation skills; where necessary, having the courage and confidence to express a point of view that is not necessarily supported by others.

- At Highfield Primary School, Plymouth, pupils from the age of six years are involved in the recruitment process for new staff. Prospective candidates join pupils and answer prepared questions in a 'circle time' format, facilitated by a classroom assistant. Pupils later share their views with the facilitator, and these inform the final decision.
- As part of West Sussex Healthy Schools Programme, a project coordinated by LEA adviser Fiona Feehan is developing political literacy. Work on preparing pupils to play an active role as citizens culminated in a simulation exercise. Pupils established a community requiring the defining of roles and responsibilities as well as the outline of those structures, laws and other processes that help to maintain and sustain a community. One of the teachers involved, Christine Davies, said:

> It was a really worthwhile project and I feel they all learnt about belonging to a community. They also learnt that they have responsibilities within their community and to their environment.

Variety of teaching methods

- The use of circle time, role play and cooperative games supports and builds upon themes of Global Citizenship. A class role play was by used by Sharon Ansell at Oakwood Special School in the West Midlands to re-enact the Brownhills Colliery disaster where 14 deaths were caused by miners breaking rules and smoking underground; 18 pupils (only one of whom had verbal language) were involved in the re-enactment, and in looking at rights and responsibilities, particularly the impact of our actions on others.

- ICT teaching methods include teleconferencing and video-conferencing. As part of a 'Global Citizenship Days' event, organised by Laura Pratt, the Buckinghamshire LEA International Officer, KS2 (P4–P7) pupils videoconferenced with others. They debated the pros and cons of the internet with a school in Sweden, and children's rights versus the rights of parents with peers in South Africa. In addition, eminent guests answered pupils' questions in live link-ups.

- Cross-curricular work is a valuable way of addressing issues of Global Citizenship. Having had a visit from the dance group Saaba, from Burkina Faso, Norma Smith, Headteacher of Lunnasting Primary School in Vidlan, Shetland said:

  > Although relating to the attainment outcomes in the Environmental Studies curriculum guidelines, I also wanted to achieve a balance of cross-curricular outcomes. Saaba's dancing and music – the initial stimulus – with their formal place in the Expressive Arts, demonstrate perfectly how learning has to be connected, particularly when in developing informed attitudes and learning to live in more sustainable ways.

Whole-school Global Citizenship initiatives and events

- Have a Global Citizenship Week. One of the five Global Citizenship themes in Chapter 3 could be followed each day, with an assembly to set the scene, and activities carried out for all or part of the day. (See Assemblies on page 44 for further ideas.) This could culminate in an event, as described below.

- Hold a Global Citizenship Evening or Open Day for parents and the local community. Encourage pupils to display work and show web sites illustrating issues of Global Citizenship, perform drama presentations, role play, songs or dances. A band or storyteller could be asked to perform (as in the example described below) and Fair Trade refreshments provided.

- The performance of a storyteller, band, drama or dance group could enliven the school. Many performers embrace issues of Global Citizenship in focusing on particular cultures or traditions, disability, anti-racism or social or environmental concerns. Some performers may themselves be disabled or homeless people or asylum seekers, and thus provide further perspectives on these issues. An Infant Department topic on Ghana at Bishop Childs Church in Wales Primary School, Cardiff, was enhanced by input from Ghanaian master drummers. The drummers inspired movement, rhythm and chanting which complemented other creative and practical work carried out.

- Invite local people into the school on a termly basis for lunch or tea, perhaps as a joint scheme with a local charity or business. There would be many jobs for pupils: writing invitations, helping to plan the menus, preparing food and taking responsibility (possibly in pairs) for one of the visitors. Perhaps extend the idea to include pupils showing the visitors their work, or inviting the visitors to a school afternoon assembly. It may be appropriate for the visitors to reciprocate. (See the Benwell Time Bank example, under 'The wider community', page 38.)

- Hold a Fair Trade Sale, or have a Fair Trade stall as part of the school fete. Enlist support by inviting a representative of fairly traded goods into the school to show what is available and to explain the philosophy to the pupils.

Governing bodies/school boards

- Attach particular governors/school board members to specific classes so that they can follow those pupils' progress through the school and become a mouthpiece for the class, reporting directly to the governing body or school board.
- Hold governors'/school board meetings at a time when people can realistically attend – daytime meetings may prevent some people from becoming involved.
- Encourage governors/school board members to attend training courses, to promote their own personal development, and enable them to contribute to taking forward school thinking.

Ethical practices

- Buy fairly traded products as far as possible. There is plenty of fairly traded tea, coffee, hot chocolate and sugar available for the staff room, plus all manner of baskets, containers, notelets and knick-knacks, for all school needs. You could even encourage the making and selling of home-made biscuits and cakes as an income-generating project for parents, or for school funds.
- Support local producers wherever possible, to strengthen the community and decrease the need for extensive transportation of goods.
- Use ethical banking for the school, for instance the Co-operative Bank.

Learning from people from diverse backgrounds and from around the world

- Schools Linking can bring great benefits and increased understanding between people, providing opportunities for schools within and between countries to interact with each other in a positive way. However, it can also present teachers and pupils with difficulties, especially if there are differing expectations on each side, unequal commitment or postal problems. See 'World links and partnerships' in Chapter 6 for further information.
- Include people who reflect the ethnic and social make-up of the area into the school when help is required – for instance, if testimonies are being sought about local history or volunteers are needed to help teachers with particular activities.
- Hold a Language Fair. Pupils at Sunnyhill Primary School, London, hold an annual Language Fair where bilingual or multilingual pupils teach words and phrases in their first language to the rest of the school. This is done through simple games such as bingo and matching pairs. This initiative can greatly raise the self-esteem of bilingual or multilingual pupils. Natasha, a Tagalog speaker, said:

> " I enjoy the Language Fair because I am happy to know that others learn a little bit of my language. The children respect us more because they see what we can do and that they can learn something from us. "

Photo 1: Language Games at Oxfam's Global Citizenship Conference, 2000 (by James Hawkins)

Even in apparently mono-cultural schools, there are likely to be children who know some of a language other than their first language, or someone locally who could teach a few words of another language, so that this type of activity could be done.

- Have a Shared Food evening, where pupils, parents, and the wider community make and share food. This could be combined with some sort of entertainment, presentation by pupils, or linked with an end-of-term celebration. You could have a theme for this, for instance healthy food, celebration food, summer food, baked food. Alternatively just ask people to cook their favourite dish, whatever that is. All of these themes encompass food from a variety of cultures.

Commitment to sustainable development

- Do Activity 6 in this chapter to develop shared thinking on sustainable development. Come up with a school policy. Undertake a joint pupil, staff and community project to promote sustainable development – what about greening a derelict area, or making an organic school garden?
- Try these ideas for staff and pupils to promote biodiversity in the school grounds:
    - grow a range of different plants and shrubs – vegetables, fruit, herbs and flowers – whatever is possible
    - put up bird boxes and bat boxes
    - grow plants, shrubs and trees which attract butterflies, such as lavender and buddleia
    - provide as many different habitats as possible – for example, a pond, a damp area, an uncultivated area for wild plants, a meadow, trees
    - avoid using pesticides or weedkillers – try alternative methods of pest control for the produce, and set up a gardening club for help with weeding and propagating.

Three Scottish primary schools in Sutherland are engaged in a UK-wide Global Footprints project to establish good practice indicators to assess how 'heavily' we tread on our planet. This has meant bringing issues of sustainable development into popular school topics such as food, energy and transport. A link has also been established with a Peruvian primary school, and work done to compare local and global issues which are of importance to each school.

Resources and displays

- Check that the world maps, atlases and globes in the school are up to date. Equal area maps such as the Peters projection, or Ekert 1V, present fairer representations of the world than the Mercator projection with its Euro-centric view. (See Chapter 5, 'maps', page 158.)

- Ensure resources you use – such as class and library books, play equipment, music collections – are free of bias and stereotyping of diversity. Dispose of some if necessary. Set up a Bias Alert! system for pupils – see Activity 5, page 24 for ideas. Buy some new books and resources which deal with issues of Global Citizenship. Your local Development Education Centre will be able to advise you (See Chapter 6 for full list).

- Build up a Global Photograph Collection. Calendars, postcards and magazines such as National Geographic can be especially useful, and can be cheaply bought at jumble sales or in charity shops. How these are used is of utmost importance – see Activity 3, page 20, for presenting positive images of people and places.

- Ensure that all displays reflect the ethos of the school.

The wider community

- Set up mutually beneficial links with people and groups in the wider community. For help and advice on the school's grounds, try the Local Agenda 21 coordinator, a local environmental group or horticultural club. In turn, the school could help the community with a local project such as transforming a local eyesore into an area of biodiversity. National organisations may well have local operations.

- Form a special link for support and learning with a local retirement or rest home, playgroup, hospice, religious establishment, prison or business. Mutually beneficial projects could be undertaken, leading to the strengthening of community feeling. An example of this is the Benwell Time Bank, based at a primary school in Newcastle. Time rather than money is exchanged for mutual benefit, through pupils and members of the community sharing skills. For instance, older people help pupils with reading, and pupils teach them computing skills.

- Mount Airey Infants School in Pembrokeshire, which has a special needs unit, has been in the forefront of consultation with the community on making improvements to an unused area of public land. The emphasis was on the rights of children to play. Pembrokeshire Development Education Centre were also involved, and a community association has been formed to further the work.

Support for staff

- Invite local experts on issues of Global Citizenship into the school – for instance, Development Education Centre staff, or local representatives of national organisations. (See Chapter 6 for contacts.)
- As a school, join organisations and associations that will increase understanding of issues of Global Citizenship. These include umbrella bodies such as the Development Education Association, Cyfanfyd, and IDEAS, or the local bodies that are members of these associations.
- There are many helpful periodicals to which the school could subscribe– see Chapter 6 for some suggestions.

For further guidance on whole-school approaches, contacts, and resources see resources in Chapter 6.

References

Brownlie, Ali (1995) *Teaching About Localities: A Development Education Approach*, Oxfam.

Burr, Margaret (1991) *We Have Always Lived Here*, Minority Rights Group.

Cardiff County Council (2000), *Local Sustainability Strategy for Cardiff*.

Clough, Nick, and Holden, Cathie (1996) 'Global Citizenship, professional competence and the chocolate cake', in *Developing the Global Teacher: Theory and Practice in Initial Teacher Education*, Steiner (ed.), Trentham Books.

Dadzie, Stella (2000) *Toolkit for Tackling Racism in Schools*, Trentham Books.

Epstein, Debbie and Sealey, Alison (1990) *Where it Really Matters*, Birmingham Development Education Centre.

Foreman, Michael (1999) *Dinosaurs and all that Rubbish*, Longman.

Gold, Jessica and Teddy (1998) *Citizens in the Classroom*, Schools Council UK.

James, Alison (1992) *Evaluating Artefacts*, Centre for Multicultural Education.

Jones, Russell (1999) *Teaching Racism Or Tackling It?: Multicultural Stories from White Beginning Teachers*, Trentham Books.

Issues in Race and Education no. 44, Spring 1985, published by the Association of London Teachers Against Racism and Fascism (ALTARF).

Mosley, Jenny (1993) *Quality Circle Time*, LDA.

Owens, Paula (2001) *Fields of Meaning*, Unpublished PhD thesis, Canterbury Christ Church University College.

Panel for Education for Sustainable Development (1999) *1998 Sustainable Education Panel First Annual Report*, DETR.

Pike, Graham and Selby, David (1988) *Global Teacher, Global Learner*, Hodder & Stoughton.

Sanders, Pete and Swinden, Liz (1990) *Knowing Me, Knowing You*, LDA.

Steiner, Miriam (1993) *Learning from Experience: Co-operative Learning and Global Education*, Trentham Books.

Steiner, Miriam (1996) 'I prefer to see myself as a global citizen', in *Developing the Global Teacher: Theory and Practice in Initial Teacher Education*, Steiner (ed.), Trentham Books.

Chapter 3
Activities to bring Global Citizenship into your school

This chapter suggests practical Global Citizenship ideas and activities for the following areas:

- Assemblies
- Foundation stage (England), Pre-5 (Scotland), Early Years (Wales)
- KS1 (England and Wales), P1–P3 (Scotland)
- KS2 (England and Wales), P4–P7 (Scotland).

We have arranged the assembly ideas and classroom activities under five Global Citizenship themes, although many of them are applicable to more than one:

1. Social justice and equity (SJE)
2. Globalisation and interdependence (G & I)
3. Appreciation of diversity (D)
4. Sustainable development (SD)
5. Peace and conflict resolution (PCR).

The ideas and activities in this chapter are designed to be taught through the principles of Global Citizenship. They will all be more effective in delivering Global Citizenship if you have explored the issues for yourself or as a whole school. Chapter 2, particularly the in-service activities section, has been written to help with this process. The activities use development education methodology. This includes active learning, cooperation, participation, interaction and inclusivity, as well as the promotion of creative and critical thinking. Many of the ideas and activities raise sensitive issues and need careful handling, and in some cases may need follow-up with individual children.

The ideas and activities in this chapter are based on the key elements for responsible citizenship set out in the diagram on pages 42–43.

Figure 3: The key elements for responsible citizenship

Social justice and equity

Understanding of inequality and injustice within and between societies. Knowledge of basic human needs and rights and of responsibilities as Global Citizens.

Critical thinking

Ability to assess viewpoints and information in an open-minded and critical way and to be able to change one's opinions, challenge one's own assumptions and make ethical judgement as a result.

Globalisation and interdependence

Knowledge about the world and its affairs: the links between countries, power relationships and different political systems. An understanding of the complexities of global issues.

Peace and conflict

Understanding of historical and present day conflicts and conflict mediation and prevention.

Ability to challenge injustice and inequalities

Ability to recognise injustice and inequality in whatever form it is met and to select appropriate action.

Skills

Ability to argue effectively

Ability to find out information and to present an informed, persuasive argument.

Knowledge and Understanding

Respect for people and things

Ability to take care of things – animate and inanimate and respond to the needs of others. Ability to make choices and recognise the consequences of choices.

Sustainable development

Knowledge of how to take care of things. A recognition that the earth's resources are finite, precious and unequally used. An understanding of the global imperative of sustainable development.

Co-operation and conflict resolution

Ability to share and work with others effectively, to analyse conflicts objectively and to find resolutions acceptable to all sides.

Diversity

Understanding of cultural and other diversity within societies and how the lives of others can enrich our own. Knowledge of the nature of prejudice towards diversity and how it can be combated.

Values and Attitudes

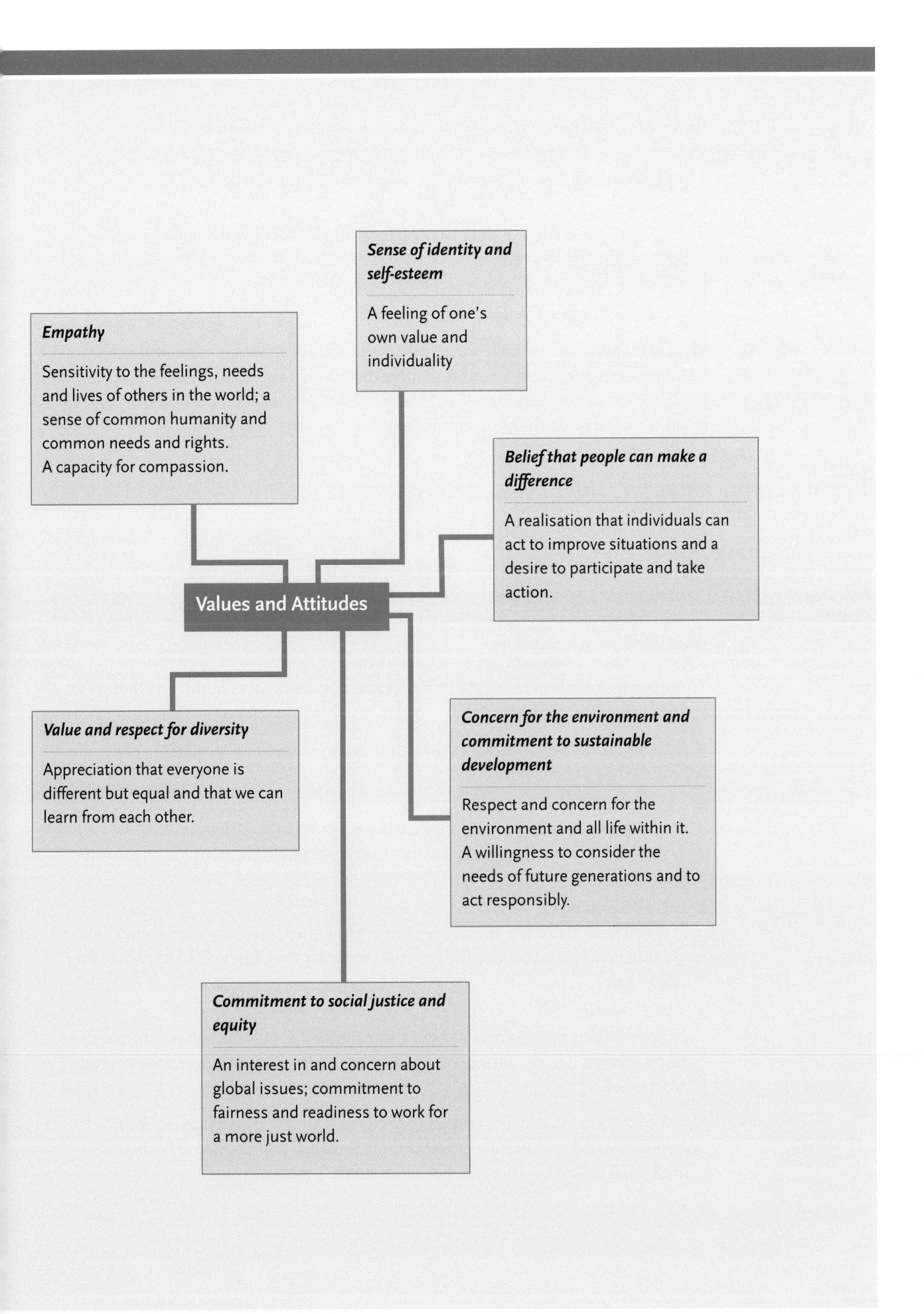

Sense of identity and self-esteem

A feeling of one's own value and individuality

Empathy

Sensitivity to the feelings, needs and lives of others in the world; a sense of common humanity and common needs and rights. A capacity for compassion.

Belief that people can make a difference

A realisation that individuals can act to improve situations and a desire to participate and take action.

Value and respect for diversity

Appreciation that everyone is different but equal and that we can learn from each other.

Concern for the environment and commitment to sustainable development

Respect and concern for the environment and all life within it. A willingness to consider the needs of future generations and to act responsibly.

Commitment to social justice and equity

An interest in and concern about global issues; commitment to fairness and readiness to work for a more just world.

Assemblies

Assemblies provide excellent opportunities for exploring issues of Global Citizenship. In this section we suggest three ways of doing this:

1. by giving a brief example of one assembly for each of the Global Citizenship themes
2. by suggesting a regular slot to look at local and global issues related to Global Citizenship in the news
3. by outlining some ideas as a starting point for developing your own school Global Citizenship Assembly Calendar.

Most of the ideas are suitable for all primary children, although some will need adapting to suit pre-fives, and you may feel that others are more suitable for older pupils. Some of the ideas could be developed into class assemblies and all of them could be followed up in the classroom.

Brief assembly ideas for Global Citizenship themes

Social justice and equity

Activity 8	Acting it out

With thanks to Annie Clews.

Aim — **To encourage pupils to think about rights and responsibilities in the way they treat, and are treated by, others.**

Ask pupils (preferably who have rehearsed) to play out several scenarios showing different kinds of behaviour.

- *First scenario*
  A new pupil in school gets lost taking the register to the office and asks for help from two other pupils. One is unkind and doesn't help the newcomer, the other does.
- *Second scenario*
  It is playtime and some friends are playing together. Another pupil comes up, wanting to join in. Some of the original group say they can't play, others say they can.
- *Third scenario*
  At lunchtime a pupil takes an apple from another pupil's lunchbox. The second pupil asks for it back: one person supports them and another backs the person who took it.

Just as each scenario is being completed, 'freeze frame' the action and ask the audience what they think each person in role feels like inside. Also ask what the injured pupil has learnt from the behaviour of the others.

Globalisation and interdependence

Activity 9 Links across the globe

Aim **To give pupils a sense of the wider world, and highlight links and connections between different places and between our lives and the lives of others.**

You will need a world map and some large, clear photographs of children in different countries around the world – on OHP transparencies if there is a large group of pupils. Ask pupils what they can see in each photograph that they recognise (and which therefore connects them to the person in the picture). For example, it could be that the person is wearing a necklace, is on a bicycle, or is playing. There will always be a connection if you look hard enough! With help from pupils, locate where each of the photographs was taken on a world map. Ask the pupils to describe any other connections they may have with the countries. For instance, they may have visited one of the countries, or have family or friends living there. Ask if anyone knows anything about any of the countries, such as the capital city, someone famous living there, or a language spoken there.

As a follow-up, in class, gather the information on post-it notes to add to one big world map showing the world links and connections from all the school.

Appreciation of diversity

Activity 10 What's my job?

Aim **To challenge stereotyped ideas and offer an alternative view.**

Invite one or two visitors who have unusual jobs into the school. Ensure they understand their role. Introduce the visitors by name, and allow three guesses from the pupils as to what job each person does. Then encourage the pupils to ask the visitors questions about their job, to which they can only answer 'yes' or 'no'. After a period of questions, or if the correct job is guessed, ask the speakers to describe their work. Classroom follow-up could focus on the difference between the initial guesses and why they might have been suggested, discussing the dangers of stereotyping and the actual job each person did. (You could ask a couple of friends to role-play this exercise if necessary.)

Sustainable development

| Activity 11 | Sustainable lifestyles – reducing waste |

Aim **To encourage children to think about their own lifestyle in our consumer society, and to reflect on how we can live in a more sustainable and less wasteful way.**

Take a selection of ordinary household 'rubbish' (suitably washed!) into assembly. Go through each item, for example, unwanted shirt, apple core, plastic bag, junk mail, empty tin, plastic yoghurt pot. Have a number of headings on view such as 'Recycle', 'Reuse', 'Refuse' (in future), 'Compost', 'Give to charity/jumble sale'. Hold each item up and ask the pupils what could be done with it. If 'reuse' is suggested, ask pupils to say what new life the item might have. (You could mention the 'Slim your bin' initiative from 'Going for Green', where one family reduced their household waste by 90 per cent in a week.)

Other ideas include:

- historical investigation – what rubbish would have been recognised by people 100 years ago?
- looking at examples of packaging – what is necessary and unnecessary? what is environmentally sound and unsound? what can we do about it?
- comparing relative amounts and types of rubbish from households here and in other countries.

Peace and conflict resolution

| Activity 12 | Cooperation! |

The poster 'The Two Mules' from *Quaker Peace & Social Witness* provided the idea for this activity. (With thanks to Lorna Jackson.)

Figure 4: The Two Mules

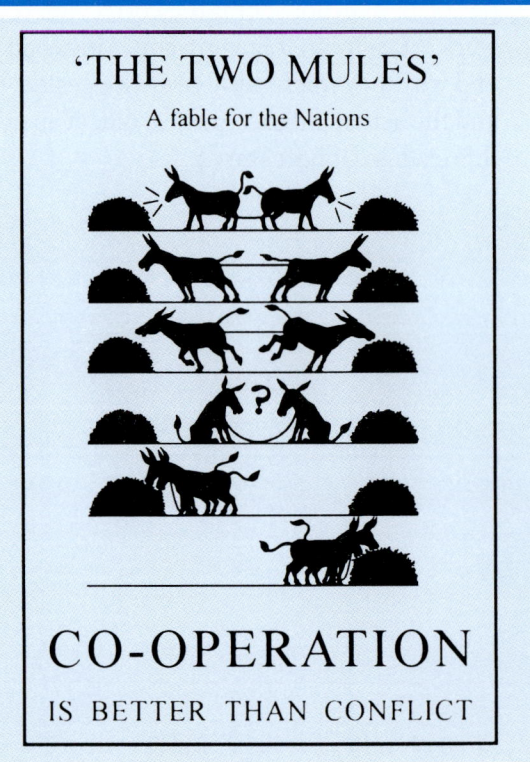

Aim **To encourage pupils to think about how difficulties can be resolved through compromise and cooperation.**

Put a PE hoop on the floor, and ask two children to stand in it, facing opposite directions. Put one apple on each side of the hoop, just out of reach. Ask the children inside the hoop to hold hands, pull in opposite directions and try to reach their apple. (Explain to them that they must not pull each other over!) Then ask other pupils to suggest why this is not a good idea, and how the children in the hoop could each reach their apples in a more cooperative way. The most obvious way is for the children to move together to pick up the apple first from one side and then from the other.

Local and global news

A regular assembly slot for local and global news provides an opportunity to present important issues to pupils in a clear way, and allows updating of ongoing issues. It also enables pupils to be involved during assembly in contributing relevant newspaper or internet articles for inclusion. Topics for such news assemblies will obviously depend on what happens, but they might include the following.

- A local issue which has caused disagreement – for instance, a new bypass, a new shopping development, the housing of asylum seekers locally, or the arrival of a community of travellers. Outline the arguments that have been given for and against – discuss these in terms of which are fact and which opinion. Ensure that there is a balance of views and that prejudices are not fuelled. Ask the pupils what they think, why, and whether these views are fact or opinion. (This could be followed up in class by asking pupils to role-play a dispute, with the rest of the class required to discuss each situation and suggest possible solutions.)

- A local or national injustice to people, animals or property – for example, damage to the school or local area, hurtful graffiti, cruelty to animals, a mugging incident, or even a murder. Explain the circumstances to the pupils and encourage them to think of ways in which such injustices can be prevented in the future.

- A current world crisis such as a war or natural disaster. Explain the reasons for different situations and focus on ways for pupils to do something positive in response. Encourage pupils to find out more about the issues. Ask them to look into the role of aid agencies and other bodies in relief work. This may lead to pupils supporting a campaign or local charity shop by donating goods or holding a sale. (Clearly, there are some issues here about raising money for charity, such as where it goes and how effective it is, and whether parents feel able to contribute. However, certainly through the right channels, money can help to alleviate suffering.)

- An annual or regular event such as the Nobel Peace Prize awards or the publication of an influential report like UNICEF's *The State of the World's Children*. This contains statistics on health and poverty worldwide. As with the last suggestion, it is important to give background and context to such work.

A Global Citizenship assembly calendar

This calendar provides ideas for celebrating specific days related to Global Citizenship throughout the year. We hope that our suggestions will give you a starting point from which you can develop ideas to suit your own educational situation. Although there are many possibilities for a calendar of this type, our selection is both small and, while all of the ideas are relevant to Global Citizenship, fairly arbitrary. The entries in the calendar are brief, and will require additional research – see Chapter 6 for further information and contacts. The last column in the calendar suggests which particular Global Citizenship theme the assembly would take, as set out at the beginning of the chapter. However, many of the ideas cover several of these themes.

We have intentionally not included religious festivals because there is a wealth of information available elsewhere already. We have also not included saints' days but certainly, there is much scope to celebrate the national saints; in the UK these are St George (23 April), St Andrew (30 November), St David (1 March) and St Patrick (17 March). There are also other important national days in every country that could be recognised, such as that to celebrate Robert Burns in Scotland (25 January).

You will see the inclusion of some celebration days that reflect the themes of Global Citizenship (marked with an asterisk). Although a particular month has been suggested for these, the dates are not set – use any which are convenient to you. Each celebration day could either be confined to assembly time, or extended for the entire day, with activities to reflect the theme. If you would like to celebrate these days, in addition to the notes given in the calendar there are many ways this could be done. Here are some suggestions.

- Use the assembly or day to concentrate on exploring one or more people, events or issues that illustrate the focus of the day.
- Draw on the school community for individuals who could give advice and enrich the assembly or day, for example, people giving testimonies, a storyteller or performer, a local expert such as a Development Education Centre worker or local NGO worker.
- Use an extended assembly or a day to run a simulation game, or have a quiz or debate.

Another idea is to roll the days into a Global Citizenship Week with events going on for all or part of each day. You could take one theme of Global Citizenship each day, such as 'social justice and equity', or 'appreciation of diversity'. Alternatively, concentrate on one topic within a theme; for example, for social justice and equity, concentrate on the UN Convention on the Rights of the Child, with a different 'right' looked at each day for a week. Alternatively, each day of the week could be used to profile five people who worked for social justice and equity.

Global Citizenship Assembly Calendar			
Assembly Date	**Assembly Topic**	**Background information and suggestions**	**Particular Global Citizenship focus**
January	Social Justice Day*	Focus on people who have worked for equity in their lifetimes, e.g. Mahatma Gandhi, Olaudah Equiano, Aung San Suu Kyi, the Dalai Lama, Mother Theresa or Nelson Mandela. Also, see Activity 8 'Acting it out' on page 44.	SJE, G & I, D, SD, PCR
3 January	Ogoni Day	International Day to celebrate the Ogoni people of West Africa. Ogoni leader and peaceful activist Ken Saro-Wiwa and others were executed in 1996 for their beliefs and actions in defending Ogoni culture, land and environment.	SJE, D, SD,
15 January	Martin Luther King Day	Focus on King's 'I have a dream' speech and ask pupils what they want the future to hold.	SJE, D, PCR
27 January	Holocaust Memorial Day	Use a children's book exploring diversity (see Chapter 6) or, for older pupils, the diary of Anne Frank as an introduction to the issues. Discuss the reasons for and consequences of xenophobia.	SJE, PCR
February	Globalisation Day*	Focus on the interdependence of countries around the world, and how this affects us in our everyday lives. See Activity 9 'Links across the globe' on page 45.	G & I, D, SD
February	Our Wonderful World Day*	Base the assembly on one or more of the 630 UNESCO World Heritage sites. 150 countries worldwide have signed an agreement to conserve these sites, which are of outstanding value. Some sites are natural and others made by human endeavour. They include Uluru-Kata Tjuta National Park in Australia (Ayers Rock), Robben Island in South Africa and the Giant's Causeway in Northern Ireland.	G & I, SD
March	All Different, All Equal Day*	See Activity 10 'What's my job', page 45 and do other work on challenging stereotypes, finding similarities between people.	SJE, D, SD, PCR
1 March	World Book Day	Share stories and poems from different traditions. Engage a storyteller or author, especially one who uses a range of languages, dialects, or accents.	SJE, G & I, D, SD, PCR
8 March	International Women's Day	Focus of the life of someone who has promoted respect and equality for women, e.g. Emmeline Pankhurst, Mary Seacole, Mary Robinson. Or invite a local businesswoman or a woman community activist to speak about her work.	SJE, G & I, SD
Second week in March every two years	Red Nose Day	Explore the reasons for the situations for which money is being raised. Show pupils examples of positive and negative media coverage linked to 'charity'. Prompt pupils to find out more about the issues.	SJE, G & I, SD

Continued overleaf

Global Citizenship Assembly Calendar *continued*			
Assembly Date	Assembly Topic	Background information and suggestions	Particular Global Citizenship focus
Second Monday in March	Commonwealth Day	Hold a world knowledge quiz about an aspect of the Commonwealth, e.g. focus on one country, or on famous people and places of the Commonwealth. Tell the pupils in advance, so that those who wish to can do some research in preparation.	G & I, D, SD
April	Disability Awareness Day*	Celebrate the achievements of a famous disabled person, e.g. David Blunkett (MP), Evelyn Glennie (musician), Professor Stephen Hawking (scientist) or Tanni Grey-Thompson (athlete). Invite a speaker to raise issues of disability with the pupils.	SJE, D, SD
April	Appropriate Technology Day*	Look at different examples of transport, house-building or toy-making around the world.	G&I, D, SD
May	Self-esteem Day*	Celebrate the achievements and talents of pupils and staff in the school, e.g. through presentations.	SJE, D, SD
Early May	International Dawn Chorus Day	Talk about the protection of bird life and bird habitats. Launch a bird survey of the grounds or local area.	SD
5 June	World Environment Day	Investigate a local or global environmental issue, perhaps with the support of the Local Agenda 21 Officer or conservation worker.	G & I, SD
End of June	Refugee Week	Focus on the difficult situation many refugees are in when they have to leave their homes quickly, or on the contribution made to our society by refugees. Invite a refugee speaker to talk to the pupils, or read a real-life testimony from a refugee or asylum seeker.	SJE, G & I, D, SD, PCR
July	Creativity Day*	Celebrate visual and performance art, drawing on a breadth of traditions.	G & I, D, SD
September	Sustainable Development Day*	See Activity 11 'Sustainable lifestyles – reducing waste' on page 46, or look at definitions of sustainable development and what they mean for children.	SD
October	Black History Month	Celebrate Black History. Contact the Local Education Authority for local initiatives. There are many influential black people in history, e.g. Cleopatra, Noor-un nisa, Inayat Khan, Mahatma Gandhi.	SJE, G & I, D, SD, PCR
16 October	World Food Day	This could introduce many facets of food: the variety of food we eat; where it comes from – the pros and cons of local and global production; healthy eating.	SJE, G & I SD
Second Monday in October	Columbus Day	A national holiday in America where there is a strong movement to refocus it as a national holiday honouring Native Americans, thus celebrating the colonised rather than the colonisers.	SJE, G & I, D, SD, PCR

Continued overleaf

Global Citizenship Assembly Calendar *continued*			
Assembly Date	**Assembly Topic**	**Background information and suggestions**	**Particular Global Citizenship focus**
Annually in October	Geography Action Week	Contact the Geographical Association for ideas and activities	SJE, G & I, D, SD, PCR
October	One World Week	Contact the organisers of One World Week for a week of educational activities and celebration of world issues following an annual theme.	SJE, G & I, D, SD, PCR
November	Indigenous People Day*	Discuss what can be learnt from the wisdom and traditions of indigenous people, and how we can support them to maintain their chosen lifestyles.	SJE, G & I, D, SD, PCR
11 November	Remembrance Day	Bring red and white (for peace) poppies and describe their significance. Read the work of a war poet. Discuss the contributions of black and Asian communities to the war effort.	SJE, G & I, D, SD, PCR
20 November	International Children's Day	Base the assembly on the Convention on the Rights of the Child. (See Chapter 4 for a list of selected articles.)	SJE, G & I, D, SD
December	Peace and Cooperation Day*	See Activity 12 'Cooperation!', page 46.	SJE, SD, PCR
1 December	World Aids Day	Challenge stereotypes and focus on practicalities: explain that you cannot contract HIV/AIDS from talking or hugging, and tell pupils what to do if they find a used needle.	SJE, G & I, D, SD
10 December	Human Rights Day	Look at the work of the UN High Commission of Human Rights, or at what the new European legislation means in practice, or focus on a particular case study.	SJE, G & I, D, SD, PCR

* Celebration days that reflect the themes of Global Citizenship

Classroom activities

Using the activities

The activities here each address aspects of Global Citizenship because their learning intentions are key elements of Global Citizenship. We have mapped the activities onto the matrices on pages 53–56 to show this.

The activities will also deliver substantial aspects of the English PSHE/Citizenship guidelines, the Welsh PSE Framework and the Scottish 5–14 Environmental Studies, 5–14 English Language and 5–14 PSD Guidelines. Each activity also has further links with other curriculum subjects. Many also promote the National Healthy Schools Scheme in England.

All of the activities are designed for everyday classroom teaching. Some may require background research, and Chapter 6 contains contacts and resources to help here. The activities can be used in any order, and can be adapted for abilities and age groups other than those suggested. They are simply examples of interesting ways to deliver aspects of the curriculum which take account of Global Citizenship. As an alternative, the activities could form the basis of a regular Global Citizenship slot or be part of a designated Global Citizenship Week. The activity headings can be used as part of long-term curriculum framework planning, and the learning intentions are useful for medium-term planning.

The timing for the activities is broadly 25–35 minutes for Foundation Stage, Pre-5/ Early Years pupils, and 40–60 minutes or longer for older pupils: in some cases work could continue over several days. (These longer activities are marked.) The majority of the activities are new, but some are 'golden oldies' from existing or out-of-date publications. Some of the activities can best be carried out in groups; for others, whole-class sessions are preferable.

The Global Citizenship curriculum outline

The following three tables show how the key elements of Global Citizenship fit across the curriculum, with progression through the year groups, and with each stage building on the last. The learning intentions are given along with the activities which deliver them.

Curriculum for Global Citizenship: knowledge and understanding

Knowledge and understanding	Foundation Stage, Pre-5/Early Years	Activities for Foundation Stage, Pre-5/Early Years	KS1 and P1–P3	Activities for KS1 and P1–P3	KS2 and P4–P7	Activities for KS2 and P4–P7
Social justice and equity	■ what is fair/unfair ■ what is right and wrong	**13** Let's make some rules **21** Dinosaurs and all that rubbish	■ awareness of rich and poor	**28** Our riches	■ fairness between groups ■ causes and effects of inequality	**50** Working children
Diversity	■ awareness of others in relation to self ■ awareness of similarities and differences between people	**14** Cooperative faces **15** A special friend **17** All in a day **19** All about me **20** What's in the shoebox?	■ greater awareness of similarities and differences between people	**30** Songlines **32** Learning about visual impairment	■ contribution of different cultures, values and beliefs to our lives ■ nature of prejudice and ways to combat it	**39** Captions! **42** Our links around the world **44** Bagchal **45** Exploring stereotypes **46** Where is this place? **47** Raising awareness of disability
Globalisation and interdependence	■ sense of immediate and local environment ■ awareness of different places	**16** We live here **17** All in a day **23** Healthy eating	■ sense of the wider world ■ links and connections between places	**30** Songlines **33** The world food restaurant	■ trade between countries ■ Fair Trade	**42** Our links around the world **43** Fair Trade **50** Working children

Continued overleaf

Curriculum for Global Citizenship: knowledge and understanding *continued*

Knowledge and understanding	Foundation Stage, Pre-5/Early Years	Activities for Foundation Stage, Pre-5/Early Years	KS1 and P1–P3	Activities for KS1 and P1–P3	KS2 and P4–P7	Activities for KS2 and P4–P7
Sustainable development	■ living things and their needs ■ how to take care of things ■ sense of future	21 Dinosaurs and all that rubbish 22 Environment watch 23 Healthy eating	■ our impact on the environment ■ awareness of the past and the future	34 Into the future 35 Sustainable living board game	■ relationship between people and environment ■ awareness of finite resources ■ our potential to change things	47 Raising awareness of disability 48 Welcome to the puppet show! 49 Sustainable living sourcebook 50 Working children 41 What is a global citizen?
Peace and conflict	■ our actions have consequences	15 A special friend 25 Tidying-up machines	■ conflicts past and present in our society and others ■ causes of conflict and conflict resolution – personal level	27 Heroes and heroines 36 Why do we fight? 38 Can I help?	■ causes of conflict ■ impact of conflict ■ strategies for tackling conflict and for conflict prevention	52 Peace and conflict in the news

Activities to bring Global Citizenship into your school • **Chapter 3** | 55

Curriculum for Global Citizenship: skills

Skills	Foundation Stage, Pre-5/Early Years	Activities for Foundation Stage, Pre-5/Early Years	KS1 and P1–P3	Activities for KS1 and P1–P3	KS2 and P4–P7	Activities for KS2 and P4–P7
Critical thinking	■ listening to others ■ asking questions	16 We live here 19 All about me 20 What's in the shoebox?	■ looking at different viewpoints ■ developing an enquiring mind	26 Challenging roles 29 Think global, act local 34 Into the future 35 Sustainable living board game 36 Why do we fight?	■ detecting bias, opinion and stereotyping ■ assessing different viewpoints	39 Captions! 45 Exploring stereotypes 46 Where is this place? 51 Investigating democracy 52 Peace and conflict in the news
Ability to argue effectively	■ expressing a view	16 We live here 20 What's in the shoebox?	■ beginning to state an opinion based on evidence	35 Sustainable living board game 37 Sunflowers	■ finding and selecting evidence ■ beginning to present a reasoned case	43 Fair Trade 48 Welcome to the puppet show! 49 Sustainable living sourcebook 51 Investigating democracy 52 Peace and conflict in the news
Ability to challenge injustice and inequalities	■ beginning to identify unfairness and take appropriate action	24 Teddy's in trouble 21 Dinosaurs and all that rubbish	■ beginning to identify unfairness and take appropriate action	26 Challenging roles 36 Why do we fight? 38 Can I help?	■ recognising and starting to challenge unfairness	39 Captions! 45 Exploring stereotypes 43 Fair Trade

Continued overleaf

Global Citizenship: The Handbook for Primary Teaching

Curriculum for Global Citizenship: skills *continued*

Skills	Foundation Stage, Pre-5/Early Years	Activities for Foundation Stage, Pre-5/Early Years	KS1 and P1–P3	Activities for KS1 and P1–P3	KS2 and P4–P7	Activities for KS2 and P4–P7
Respect for people and things	■ starting to take care of things – animate and inanimate ■ starting to think of others	25 Tidying-up machines	■ empathising and responding to the needs of others ■ making links between our lives and the lives of others ■ learning about visual impairment	27 Heroes and heroines 33 The world food restaurant 29 Think global, act local 36 Why do we fight? 37 Sunflowers 38 Can I help?	■ making choices and recognising the consequences of choices	43 Fair Trade 44 Bagchal 48 Welcome to the puppet show! 50 Working children
Cooperation and conflict resolution	■ cooperation ■ sharing ■ starting to look at resolving arguments peacefully ■ starting to participate	14 Cooperative faces 24 Teddy's in trouble 25 Tidying-up machine	■ tact and diplomacy ■ involving and including society and others	38 Can I help? 32 Learning about visual impairment	■ accepting and acting on group decisions ■ compromising	48 Welcome to the puppet show! 52 Peace and conflict in the news 41 What is a global citizen?

Curriculum for Global Citizenship: values and attitudes

Values and attitudes	Foundation Stage, Pre-5/Early Years	Activities for Foundation Stage, Pre-5/Early Years	KS1 and P1–P3	Activities for KS1 and P1–P3	KS2 and P4–P7	Activities for KS2 and P4–P7
Sense of identity and self-esteem	■ sense of identity and self-worth	**18** Multilingual catch **19** All about me **20** What's in the shoebox?	■ awareness of and pride in individuality	**31** A recipe for myself **37** Sunflowers	■ sense of importance of individual worth	**41** What is a global citizen? **48** Welcome to the puppet show! **51** Investigating democracy
Empathy and sense of common humanity	■ concern for others in immediate circle	**15** A special friend	■ interest and concern for others in wider sphere	**32** Learning about visual impairment	■ empathy towards others locally and globally	**40** Homelessness **46** Where is this place? **47** Raising awareness of disability
Commitment to social justice and equity	■ sense of fair play	**21** Dinosaurs and all that Rubbish **24** Teddy's in trouble	■ sense of personal indignation ■ willingness to speak up for others	**26** Challenging roles **28** Our riches	■ growing interest in world events ■ sense of justice	**42** Our links around the world **39** Captions! **52** Peace and conflict in the news
Valuing and respecting diversity	■ positive attitude towards difference and diversity	**14** Cooperative faces **17** All in a day **18** Multilingual catch	■ valuing others as equal and different ■ willingness to learn from the experiences of others	**27** Heroes and heroines **30** Songlines **31** A recipe for myself **38** Can I help?	■ growing respect for difference and diversity	**44** Bagchal **47** Raising awareness of disability **41** What is a global citizen?

Continued overleaf

Curriculum for Global Citizenship: values and attitudes *continued*

Values and attitudes	Foundation Stage, Pre-5/Early Years	Activities for Foundation Stage, Pre-5/Early Years	KS1 and P1–P3	Activities for KS1 and P1–P3	KS2 and P4–P7	Activities for KS2 and P4–P7
Concern for the environment and commitment to sustainable development	■ appreciation of own environment and living things ■ sense of wonder and curiosity	**16** We live here **21** Dinosaurs and all that rubbish **22** Environment watch	■ concern for the wider environment ■ beginning to value resources ■ willingness to care for the environment	**34** Into the future **35** Sustainable living board game	■ sense of responsibility for the environment and the use of resources	**49** Sustainable living sourcebook
Belief that people can make a difference	■ willingness to admit to and learn from mistakes	**24** Teddy's in trouble	■ awareness that our actions have consequences ■ willingness to cooperate and participate	**29** Think global, act local **34** Into the future **36** Why do we fight?	■ belief that things can be better and that individuals can make a difference	**40** Homelessness **43** Fair Trade **48** Welcome to the puppet show! **51** Investigating democracy **41** What is a global citizen?

Foundation Stage (England), Pre-5 (Scotland)/ Early Years (Wales)

These activities will take approximately 25–35 minutes, unless otherwise stated.

Links are made to the Early Learning Goals in England, the Curriculum Framework 3–5 in Scotland, and the Desirable Outcomes for Children's Learning Before Compulsory School Age in Wales.

Social justice and equity

Activity 13 Let's make some rules!

Learning intention For pupils to understand what is fair and unfair, right and wrong.

Resources
- pictures illustrating unfair behaviour
- paper and crayons/paints

Activity Talk to pupils about the kinds of behaviour in school that are fair and unfair, using the pictures as a stimulus. Encourage the pupils to suggest some class behaviour 'rules', which everyone will try to stick to. Display these rules and pupils' accompanying pictures and read them regularly to remind the children. (This activity could be extended if all the classes drew up their class rules, and compared and discussed them at an assembly resulting in an agreed set of 'School's rules'.)

Planned outcome That pupils understand that they can contribute to the class, and become aware of class rules and the importance of trying to keep them.

Curriculum links

England	Scotland	Wales
Personal, social and emotional development; knowledge of the world	Emotional, personal and social development; communication and language; knowledge and understanding of the world	Personal and social development; knowledge and understanding of the world; language, literacy and communication skills

Activity 14 Cooperative faces

This activity is from *Learning Together* by Susan Fountain.

Learning intention **For pupils to gain an awareness of similarities and differences between people, develop a positive attitude towards difference and diversity, and cooperate with others.**

Resources
- four photographs of the faces of children from different genders and ethnic backgrounds cut into three pieces, mixed up and put into four envelopes
- one tray

Activity For four players. Give each player an envelope and tell them they have to make four faces within their group. They look in their envelopes, and put any unwanted shapes in a tray in the middle, to be taken by others. When completed, ask: how are the faces similar/different? How did you know whether the person was a boy or a girl?

	Planned outcome	That pupils appreciate that people are different but equal, and work cooperatively.

Curriculum links

England	Scotland	Wales
Personal, social and emotional development; knowledge and understanding of the world; physical development	Emotional, personal and social development; Knowledge and understanding of the world	Personal and social development; knowledge and understanding of the world

Activity 15   A special friend

Learning intention For pupils to have an awareness of others in relation to themselves, appreciate that their actions have consequences, and show concern for others in their immediate circle

Resources
- a book that illustrates friendship, such as *Aldo* by John Burningham
- paper, glue, scissors and materials for collage

Activity Read the book with the pupils and then talk about what they do when they are feeling sad or lonely and how class members can help each other at these times. Talk about what makes a friend, what friends do for each other and how to be friendly to new children in the class. Think about particular words to describe friends, about times when we fall out with friends and how to become friends again. Discuss times when pupils like being or want to be on their own. As an extension, pupils could to make collages of themselves with their 'special friend', or make a picture for someone special to them.

Planned outcome That pupils understand the value of friendship.

Curriculum links

England	Scotland	Wales
Personal, social and emotional development	Emotional, personal and social development; communication and language	Personal and social development; language, literacy and communication skills

Globalisation and interdependence

Activity 16   We live here

Learning intention **For pupils to gain a sense of immediate and local environment, to be able to express a view and listen to others.**

Resources
- simple jigsaws made from two identical photographs of the local area (see photo 2) – one kept whole as a guide, the other stuck on card and cut up into pieces (photographs from a local newspaper would be suitable)

Activity Show the pupils the whole photographs (those kept as the guide), and talk about where the places are, what happens there, who lives nearby. Introduce the word 'local'. Then give the pupils the jigsaws to complete.

Planned outcome That pupils gain an increased awareness of the local area.

Photo 2: Whitehaven Docks (by Gisela Renolds)

Curriculum links

England	Scotland	Wales
Knowledge and understanding of the world; physical development	Knowledge and understanding of the world	Knowledge and understanding of the world

Activity 17   All in a day

Learning intention   For pupils to gain an awareness of similarities and differences between people, an awareness of different places, and a positive attitude towards difference and diversity.

Resources
- a book showing everyday lives around the world, such as *Shompa Lives in India* by Jean Harrison, *Wake up World!* by Beatrice Hollyer or *Your World, My World* by Teresa Garlake.
- paper and crayons/paints

Activity   Look at and talk about similarities between the daily lives of those in the books and our own lives. Ask the pupils to illustrate a frieze entitled 'A day in the life of our class'.

Planned outcome   That pupils become more aware of the similarities between people around the world.

Note: *Shompa Lives in India can also be used for work on Diwali, because Shompa and her family are Hindu.*

Curriculum links

England	Scotland	Wales
Personal, social and emotional development; knowledge and understanding of the world; creative development	Knowledge and understanding of the world; emotional, personal and social development	Language, literacy and communication skills; personal and social development; knowledge and understanding of the world; creative development

Activity 18   Multilingual catch

Learning intention: **For pupils to gain a sense of identity and self-worth, and a positive attitude towards difference and diversity.**

Resources:
- a beanbag

Activity: Teach pupils to count to three or to say some words in a language perhaps new to some of them, such as Hindi, Twi, Spanish, Welsh (draw on the skills of the pupils!). Practise the words by throwing a beanbag around a circle and asking the catcher to repeat one, two, and three, or a word in the new language before throwing the beanbag to someone else.

Planned outcome: For pupils to be proud of themselves and to appreciate that there are different languages in the world and that they can learn them.

Curriculum links:

England	Scotland	Wales
Personal, social and emotional development; knowledge and understanding of the world; physical development	Communication and language; knowledge and understanding of the world	Language, literacy and communication skills; personal and social development; knowledge and understanding of the world; physical development

Appreciation of diversity

Activity 19   All about me

This activity is adapted from *Developing Circle Time* by Teresa Bliss, George Robinson and Barbara Maines.

Learning intention: **That pupils become aware of similarities and differences between people, that they listen to others, and gain a sense of identity and self-worth.**

Note: Although we have given an example of a circle time activity here, it is a technique which has certain conventions and we would recommend further reading on it. (See Chapter 6, Peace and Conflict Resolution, Activities and Resources.)

Activity: Within sharing or circle time, suggest the beginning of one of the following sentences and ask each pupil to finish it:
- 'I am special because …'
- 'Something I really like is …'
- 'A time I was brave was …'
- 'Something that makes me happy/sad/cross/upset is …'.

Planned outcome: That pupils will have listened to and learnt about others, and increased their confidence in speaking and expressing themselves.

Activities to bring Global Citizenship into your school • Chapter 3

Curriculum links

England	Scotland	Wales
Personal, social and emotional development; language and communication; creative development	Emotional, personal and social development; communication and language	Language, literacy and communication skills; personal and social development

Activity 20 What's in the shoebox?

This activity could continue as a short slot over several weeks.

Learning intention For pupils to listen to others, ask questions, express a view, feel a sense of identity and self-worth, and gain an awareness of others in relation to themselves.

Resources
- a shoebox
- classroom toys
- art materials

Activity Explain to the class that everyone will be having a go at playing a guessing game where each person thinks of their favourite colour, animal, food and toy, and the others have to try to guess what they are. One child at a time secretly finds representations of these favourite things around the classroom – for instance, a model of their favourite animal, or their favourite colour as a crayon, or they could do drawings of these things. These are then put into a special shoebox. At sharing time, the person who has chosen sits with the shoebox, and gives clues as to what the things are. The others try to guess, and when a correct guess has been made, the object can be shown.

Planned outcome To enhance pupils' self-esteem, and enable them to have fun while promoting their speaking and listening skills.

Curriculum links

England	Scotland	Wales
Personal, social and emotional development	Emotional, personal and social development; communication and language	Language, literacy and communication skills; personal and social development

Sustainable development

Activity 21 Dinosaurs and all that rubbish

Learning intention For pupils to gain a sense of the future, begin to identify unfairness, and have an appreciation of their own environment and of living things.

Resources
- book: *Dinosaurs and all that Rubbish* by Michael Foreman

Global Citizenship: The Handbook for Primary Teaching

Activity Read the story to the class and then ask:

- was the man right to make such a mess and then just leave it?
- was the man right to say everything belonged to him when he came back?
- what did he learn from the dinosaurs?
- what can we learn from this story?

Role-play short extracts of the story. Follow up by talking about how to take care of things in the classroom. Ask pupils to identify what needs tidying up. (See Activity 25 'Tidying-up machines' on page 66.)

Planned outcome That pupils begin to learn that we all have responsibilities towards the Earth.

Curriculum links

England	Scotland	Wales
Language and communication; knowledge and understanding of the world	Knowledge and understanding of the world; communication and language	Language, literacy and communication skills; personal and social development; knowledge and understanding of the world

Activity 22   Environment watch

This activity will take longer than one session.

Learning intention **For pupils to gain knowledge and understanding of the needs of living things, and how to take care of them, to have a sense of the future, and to feel wonder and curiosity about their environment.**

Resources
- paper
- clipboards for adults
- crayons/paints
- seeds/seedlings, earth trays, water, small gardening tools or domestic forks

Activity Take the pupils on a local walk or around the school grounds. Ask them to collect data (with help from adults) on things they like and don't like, such as trees, flower-beds, rubbish and dog dirt. On return to the classroom, talk about their likes and dislikes, and ask the pupils what they would like to see in the future. Encourage them to draw pictures about their likes or dislikes, and write a sentence to support them. Send the work to the head teacher (for school grounds) or local council (for local walk) with a covering letter outlining areas of pupils' support and concern. As a further activity, encourage pupils to plant and care for flower seeds and to cultivate tree seedlings with a view to adding them to the school grounds or offering them to a municipal garden. Attract wider concern by telling the story to the local paper.

Planned outcome That pupils become more aware of their locality, and begin to see how they can have an effect on it, and appreciate plants and learn about how to grow them.

Curriculum links

England	Scotland	Wales
Personal, social and emotional development; language and communication; knowledge and understanding of the world; creative development	Emotional, personal and social development; knowledge and understanding of the world	Language, literacy and communication skills; personal and social development; knowledge and understanding of the world

Activity 23   Healthy eating

Learning intention For pupils to gain an awareness of different places, an appreciation of their local environment, and to understand the needs of living things.

Resources
- box of fruit and vegetables
- paper, glue, scissors and materials for collage
- if possible, different types of waste paper, plastic and straw from a greengrocer's packing materials

Activity Take a box of fruit and vegetables into the class. Try to get a variety of locally produced (or at least within the country), grown abroad, and unfamiliar fruit and vegetables. Encourage the pupils to look at, handle, and name everything. Ask them where they think each piece comes from, and how it might get here – introduce the words 'local' and 'global' or 'near' and 'far'. Give pupils the opportunity to taste the fruit and vegetables. Ask them to make collages of the produce for a class 'healthy eating' display.

Planned outcome For pupils to learn that fruit and vegetables come from different places, and that they are healthy foods.

Link This healthy eating game adds fun to the activity. Sit the pupils in a circle, and name them 'Paw-paw', 'Apple', 'Yam' and 'Turnip', repeated all round (any healthy food that links with your topic can be chosen.) When you say 'apple', all the Apples get up and change places with each other; similarly for the other names. If you say 'fruit' the Apples and Paw-paws change, and likewise for 'veg'. For the whole group to swap places (and cause some chaos!) simply shout, 'healthy eating'!

Note: *This activity could be done at milk time, with one fruit or vegetable introduced each day.*

Curriculum links

England	Scotland	Wales
Knowledge and understanding of the world; creative development; physical development	Knowledge and understanding of the world; physical development and movement; expressive and aesthetic development	Language, literacy and communication skills; personal and social development; knowledge and understanding of the world; physical development; creative development

Global Citizenship: The Handbook for Primary Teaching

Peace and conflict resolution

Activity 24 Teddy's in trouble

Learning intention For pupils to start to participate, develop a sense of fair play and a willingness to admit to and learn from mistakes, beginning to identify unfairness and take appropriate action.

Resources
- glove-puppet or toy

Activity Using a glove-puppet or class toy as the focus, talk about personal incidents that occur in school, and ask the pupils to suggest what to do. For example, Teddy can't remember what to do if he or she wants to go to the toilet – can anyone help? (Ask the teacher.) Teddy was fighting in the playground today – can anyone remind help him or her what to do? (Tell a teacher or peer mediator about problems rather than fight.)

Planned outcome For pupils to understand that they can make mistakes and forget things, but that they can learn from these mistakes and that others around them can help.

Curriculum links

England	Scotland	Wales
Personal, social and emotional development; language and communication	Emotional, personal and social development; communication and language	Language, literacy and communication skills; personal and social development

Activity 25 Tidying-up machines

Learning intention For pupils to understand the need to take care of inanimate things, to cooperate within the class, and be aware that their actions have consequences.

Activity Ask pupils about the jobs that need to be done in the classroom or in a shared work area to keep it tidy. Allocate a job to a group of four, asking the pupils to use their bodies as a machine to do the job! They must all be touching in some way and all have a role. Perhaps ask them to invent a noise for their machine (if you can stand it!).

Planned outcome That pupils begin to take responsibility for their classroom environment, learn to be creative and cooperative, and have fun while tidying.

Curriculum links

England	Scotland	Wales
Personal, social and emotional development; physical development; language and communication	Physical development and movement; emotional, personal and social development; communication and language	Language, literacy and communication skills; personal and social development; physical development

KS1 (England and Wales), P1–P3 (Scotland)

Most of these activities will take between 40 and 60 minutes. The others, which are marked, will take a half-day or a whole day or even longer. Most can be extended into longer activities if desired. We have also noted where we feel activities are best suited to the top end of the age group. The activities here each address aspects of Global Citizenship: you can see which aspects by looking at the learning intentions at the start of each activity. (Also see mapping on pages 53–58.)

The activities will also deliver substantial aspects of the English PSHE/Citizenship Guidelines, the Welsh PSE Framework, and the Scottish 5–14 Environmental Studies, 5–14 English Language and 5–14 PSD Guidelines. Each activity also has further links with other English, Welsh and Scottish curriculum subjects. These links are shown in the table beneath each activity. Most curriculum references are relevant for Wales as well as England, and specific references to the Welsh National Curriculum are highlighted. Many of the activities also promote the National Healthy Schools Scheme in England.

Social justice and equity

Activity 26 Challenging roles

This is a role-play idea adapted from *Global Teacher, Global Learner* by Graham Pike and David Selby.

Learning intention For pupils to look at different viewpoints, develop an enquiring mind, begin to identify unfairness, and develop a willingness to speak up for others.

Activity Ask the pupils what they think a teacher/librarian/nurse is like. Sensitively challenge any stereotypes or generalisations that might arise, by asking, for example, if *all* nurses are like that, or if *all* teachers would say that. Suggest 'unexpected' situations to groups of pupils, such as a police officer who is caught shoplifting, a painter and decorator who is afraid of heights, a soldier who doesn't agree with the war. Ask the pupils to think up other ideas. Ask each group to act out a brief scene involving the character. After each one, centre class discussion on what they would have expected of the character, and why. As a follow-up, use pictures of men and women in unexpected roles to underline that assumptions and stereotypes can be unfair and wrong.

Planned outcomes That pupils begin to understand the need to question assumptions and stereotypes.

Curriculum links

England	Scotland	Wales
PSHE/Citizenship: to recognise what is right and wrong; to recognise, name and deal with their feelings in a positive way; to identify and respect the differences and similarities of others **Literacy Hour:** Year 1, term 2	**PSD:** interpersonal relationships; to evaluate the relationships they and society hold **Environmental Studies:** to develop informed attitudes; cultural and social diversity **Expressive Arts:** development of positive attitude to self and others **English Language:** talking about feelings, opinions	**PSE:** to respect others and value their achievements **Oracy:** using talk to develop their thinking by exploring, developing and clarifying ideas

Activity 27 Heroes and heroines in the hot seat (Upper KS1/P3)

Learning intention For pupils to investigate conflicts, past and present, in our society and others, to make links between our lives and the lives of others, and to be willing to learn from the experiences of others.

Resources
- a limited amount of information (mainly pictures with captions) about people whose lives were dedicated to social justice and equity (see Global Citizenship Assembly Calendar, on page 49 for some ideas)

Activity Divide the pupils into groups of four or five, and ask each group to choose one person, then find out as much as possible about the person's life. Then ask each group to think up five questions which they would like to ask about the person's life. Bring the class together and ask one child from each group to sit in the 'hot seat' and 'be' the person they have researched. They answer the questions from their own group, which results in their presenting an outline of the person's life to the class.

Planned outcome Pupils appreciate that there have been many influential people in history committed to social justice and equity, who made a difference in their lifetime and from whom we can learn.

Curriculum links

England	Scotland	Wales
PSHE/Citizenship: to listen to other people and work cooperatively; to take and share responsibility; how to set simple goals; to consider simple political issues (why are some historical figures remembered more than others? how were they treated during their lifetime?) **History:** the lives of famous people **Literacy Hour:** Year 1, term 3	**PSD:** active experiential learning **Environmental Studies:** people in the past; why certain people are regarded as significant; people in society; rights and responsibilities; conflict and decision making **RME:** appreciate moral values such as liberty and justice	**PSE:** to be curious and inquisitive and have a sense of wonder; to respect others and value their achievements **Oracy:** to speak with confidence; to incorporate relevant detail in explanations

Activity 28 Our riches

Learning intention For pupils to gain an awareness of rich and poor and a sense of personal indignation.

Resources
- Copy of this quotation up in the classroom for everyone to see:
  > Only when the last tree has died and the last river been poisoned and the last fish been caught will we realise that we cannot eat money.
  > *Native American Cree saying*

Alternatively, if you prefer, use a book such as *The Selfish Giant* by Oscar Wilde or a simplified version of *A Christmas Carol* by Charles Dickens.

Activity Show the pupils the quotation above, attributed to the Native American Cree as a comment on the environment and materialism, or read one of the books. Discuss its meaning and implications with the class. Divide the board in half vertically and write

'Rich' one side and 'Poor' the other. Ask the pupils for their ideas on these two terms. Initially they will probably focus on money and material wealth, but broaden the discussion to ensure that all aspects of the terms rich and poor are discussed: richness in terms of friends, happiness, culture or seeing a beautiful view, for instance. 'Poor' should include poverty of experiences or opportunities, such as never going out or doing anything exciting, and having a polluted environment.

Talk about how the pupils, and many people throughout the world, are both rich and poor. For instance, in this country a family may have a car but one of them may also have asthma, whereas in Bhutan, Asia, a family may not have a car but they do have a beautiful, clean environment. Ask pupils to record how they are each rich and poor as pictures and captions for a class book.

Planned outcome That pupils begin to understand ways in which they are 'rich' and 'poor' and that there is value in things apart from money and materialism.

Curriculum links

England	Scotland	Wales
PSHE/Citizenship: to share their opinions on things that matter to them and explain their views; to realise that they belong to various groups and communities such as families; to take part in discussions of global concern	**PSD:** self-esteem – to express positive thoughts about themselves	**PSE:** to value friends and families as a source of love and mutual support; to feel positive about themselves

Globalisation and interdependence

Activity 29 Think global, act local

Learning intention For pupils to look at different viewpoints, develop an enquiring mind, empathise with and respond to the needs of others, and become aware that our actions have consequences.

Resources
- paper
- clipboards
- post-it notes
- card and crayons/paints

Activity Organise a trip to a local farm, a food producer, a farmer's market or to a local vegetable box scheme. Encourage pupils to find out as much as possible about locally produced products. For instance:
- What varieties of fruit and vegetables are grown?
- How is the cheese produced?
- How does the farmer or producer look after their land?
- Is the production organic?

Ask about the difficulties faced by the farmer or producer. If possible, tour the site and ask pupils (with help from adults if necessary) to annotate a simple map. Buy some of the produce and, if appropriate, ask the pupils to collect some natural objects such as fallen leaves, twigs and stones, for a display, but ensure that pupils don't pick flowers. Back at school, give each pair of pupils two post-it notes, asking them to write three reasons for buying local produce on one note, and three reasons for buying produce from abroad on the other. Draw a vertical line down the board, with two headings, 'Local' and 'Global'. Ask pupils to add their papers and discuss the issues together. Make thank-you cards for the host of your visit, including some of the pupil's comments in support of local produce. Artwork of the produce could also be included with the letter.

Planned outcome That pupils realise where produce can come from, and understand some simple issues about local and global supply, and some of the difficulties faced by food producers.

Curriculum links

England	Scotland	Wales
PSHE/Citizenship: what improves and harms the local natural environment and how people look after it; to make real choices; to meet and talk with people; to consider simple environmental issues **Art and Design:** recording from first-hand observation of natural objects **ICT:** writing simple sentences, and creating pictures (for thank-you cards) **Science:** plants and animals in the local environment	**PSD:** to reflect on the needs of others in relation to self; positive regard for others **Environmental studies:** developing informed attitudes, local and global; responsible use of the natural environment in accordance with the principles of sustainability **Science:** developing an understanding of the interdependence of living things with the environment	**PSE:** concern about the environment; knowledge about features in the local environment **Science:** living things in their environment

Activity 30   Songlines

Learning intention For pupils to have a greater awareness of similarities and differences between people, and the links and connections between places, and to be willing to learn from the experiences of others.

Resources
- information about songlines
- photographs showing a range of different landscapes and physical features, such as forest, desert, a river, ice caps, mountains, a bridge, a gate, a building
- simple musical instruments for everyone
- a book such as *Panda's Puzzle*, by Michael Foreman

Activity	Sitting in a circle, tell the children about Songlines.
	> The Australian Aborigines have turned their journeys into songs. Using 'Songlines', they can trace their way across huge expanses of desert, finding water, food and shelter from the information in their songs. Songlines are inherited journeys – different songs belong to different families and as well as having lots of up-to-date information, the stories in the songs also explain how that stretch of land was shaped long ago when the Dreamtime Ancestors were awake and walking across the country. So, an Aboriginal Songline gives people both 'physical' and 'spiritual' maps of the land they live on.
	From Talking to the Earth *by Gordon MacLellan*
	Read the story and show the pupils the photographs to set the scene for an imaginary journey the pupils will undertake. Go around the class asking each person to say a place or a physical feature that could be seen on a journey, for example 'the sea', 'the bridge'. The children need to remember what they have said. Go around the circle again asking pupils to add a brief description, such as 'I went over the swirling and wavy sea' or 'I went under the huge metal bridge'. Give out the musical instruments, and ask pupils to think of a musical pattern to accompany their phrase. Go around the circle again, with each individual in turn saying their phrase and accompanying themselves with their musical pattern. Finally, only the musical pattern is played. Perhaps you could tape this to play back to the class later, or use it for a class assembly.
Planned outcome	That pupils understand the idea of songlines, and have had fun and used their imaginations in creating their own.
Curriculum links	

England	Scotland	Wales
PSHE/Citizenship: to contribute to the life of the class and school; to listen to other people; to play and work cooperatively **Music:** exploring sounds **Science:** sound and hearing	**PSD:** interpersonal relationships **Environmental Studies:** developing an understanding of distinctive features of life in the past and why certain societies, people and events are regarded as significant	**PSE:** to recognise and value cultural differences and diversity **Music:** to create, select and organise sounds in response to different stimuli **Science:** life processes

Appreciation of diversity

Activity 31   A recipe for myself

	This activity is adapted from *Feeling Good About Faraway Friends* published by Leeds Development Education Centre.
Learning intention	**For pupils to become aware of and have pride in their individuality, and that they value others as equal and different.**
Resources	■ paper and pencils

Activity Create a word bank by brainstorming other pupils' qualities: funny, helpful, talkative, stubborn, and so on. Ask pupils to choose words which they think describe themselves and write them as a recipe. Encourage pupils to see themselves positively, for example, 2 cupfuls of fun, a pinch of mischief. Make a class book of recipes.

Planned outcome That pupils see themselves positively, that their self-esteem is raised, and that they begin to realise that people are all different, but all equal.

Figure 5: Recipe book

TRISH

Ingredients
2 cups of laughter
1 cup of joy
1 cup of energy
a sprinkle of tears
a pinch of stubborness
a dash of playfulness

Method
Stand under the stars and growing moon for several nights. Bring into a warm and secure place, nurture with love and care, and watch it grow into Trish

Curriculum links

England	Scotland	Wales
PSHE/Citizenship: to recognise what they like and dislike; to think about themselves and recognise what they are good at; to feel positive about themselves; to identify and respect differences and similarities between people. **Literacy Hour:** Year 1, term 1; Year 2, term 1 **Science:** ourselves **ICT:** using a word bank	**PSD:** positive regard for self and for others and their needs **Environmental Studies:** developing informed attitudes, cultural and social diversity **Health:** feelings and relationships and how they affect our mental well-being **English Language:** talking about feelings	**PSE:** to feel positive about themselves; to know that each person is different but understand that all are equal in value **Oracy:** to extend their vocabulary through activities that encourage their interest in words **Science:** humans and other animals

Global Citizenship: The Handbook for Primary Teaching

Activity 32   Learning about visual impairment

This activity requires two sessions.

Learning intention For pupils to become aware of the similarities and differences between people, to empathise with the needs of others and have an interest in, and concern for, others in the wider sphere and to acquire skills of tact, and diplomacy.

Resources
- information from the RNIB, or The Guide Dogs for the Blind Association who provide the story of a guide dog, and the dos and don'ts when seeing a working guide dog in the street

Activity: Session 1 Share the information with the whole class, including reading the guide dog story, and discuss some of the issues raised. Ask the pupils, in twos, to write some questions they would like to ask a visitor who has an understanding of the issues. The visitor could be a teacher of the blind, a guide dog user, or a local support group spokesperson. Discuss the questions as a class group, and together decide on about six or seven that encompass the main queries without duplication. You may need to challenge some stereotypes. (See Chapter 2 page 29, Activity 7 on visitors.)

Activity: Session 2 Invite a visitor in. Encourage the pupils to ask the visitor the prepared questions. Also ask the visitor to suggest ways pupils could be helpful to visually impaired people in their daily lives, as well as telling pupils about particular devices visually impaired people use to help themselves. Plan a class assembly to tell other pupils what the class has learnt.

Note: *Be aware of the Health and Safety issues if a guide dog comes into school.*

Planned outcome That pupils begin to learn about issues of visual impairment, including that people are affected to different degrees, that such people are different but equal to themselves, and that there are things they can do to help.

Curriculum links

England	Scotland	Wales
PSHE/Citizenship: to realise that people and other living things have needs, and that they have responsibilities to meet them; to meet and talk with people; to ask for help (in understanding the needs of visually impaired people)	**PSD:** to reflect on attitudes towards others; the needs of others in relation to self	**PSE:** to show care and consideration for others; to be willing to help others
	Environmental Studies: people and needs; rights and responsibilities; equality of opportunity	**Oracy:** to speak with confidence; to respond appropriately and effectively to what they have heard
Literacy Hour: Year 2, term 1		**Science:** life processes
Science: ourselves		

Activity 33   The world food restaurant

This activity requires two longish sessions. The home corner can be set up for as long as you wish.

Learning intention For pupils to gain a sense of the wider world and make links between different places and between our lives and the lives of others.

Resources: Session 1
- a world map
- magazines
- scissors, blu-tac, pencils, paper
- prepared sheets

For the prepared sheets choose a number of staple foods eaten around the world, such as pasta, rice, potatoes, breads, maize. Write the name of each of the foods as a title on a large sheet of paper. Stick some photographs and recipes showing different ways these staples are eaten on the appropriate sheets. You will also need some examples of the staple foods for tasting, and a sample of writing from a newspaper food critic.

Activity: Session 1 With the whole class, discuss the versatility of the staple foods using the prepared sheets to show the types of meals that can be made with them. Then give the pupils a few pages from magazines to cut up, so that they can add other meals made of the same staple foods to the appropriate sheets. (It would be best to use blu-tac in case they need to be moved.) Talk about the nutritional value of the staples. Ask the pupils to help you locate on a world map where the staple foods are most commonly grown and eaten. Discuss why there is a correlation. Give pupils the opportunity to taste some of the staple foods, and to say if and where they have had them before. Read out the food critic's piece and ask pupils to write in the same style about any food tried in class.

Resources: Session 2
- paper and paints for printing
- some items for printing from, such as used fast-food packaging, modelling materials

Activity: Session 2 Talk about the variety of local restaurants and fast-food outlets, mentioning the issue of disposable packaging, and asking pupils for their thoughts on this. Talk about the hygiene required for handling food in a restaurant.

Suggest setting up a 'world food restaurant' in the home corner and talk about what it would serve. Discuss different requirements for particular people, including vegetarians or vegans, diabetics, people who are recovering from illness and may only want something very light to eat. Ask pupils to design a product that would encourage children to eat more fruit or vegetables. Ask pupils to write the food choices, design the menus and give the prices, bearing the discussions in mind. Where possible, encourage the use of dual-language texts. For ongoing work in creating the world food restaurant, pupils can make food out of papier maché, plasticine, or other materials, display their menus, and write food poems to decorate the restaurant. Enable pupils to print decorative borders round the menus and poems using scrunched up packaging, plastic bottles, or food shapes cut out from used polystyrene containers. Clearly, real food can also be used – but in this case, do printing in groups by turn, to minimise waste.

Planned outcome For pupils to appreciate that there is great diversity of ways in which foods can be prepared, that different nationalities have learnt a lot from each other in this regard, and that many staple foods have similar nutritional value.

Curriculum links

England	Scotland	Wales
PSHE/Citizenship: how to make simple choices that improve their health and well-being; to maintain personal hygiene; to develop relationships through work and play **ICT:** understanding instructions, following sequences **Maths:** work involving calculating the costs of various meals, weights and measures **Science:** health and growth **RE:** cooking for a religious celebration **Art and Design:** printing using different materials, making decorative posters **D & T:** to design and make a product for a particular occasion or group; to encourage children to eat more fruit or vegetables	**PSD:** positive regard for others **RME:** differences are seen as welcome enrichments **Environmental Studies:** developing informed attitudes; importance of interdependence **Maths:** work involving calculating the costs of various meals, weights and measures	**PSE:** to know that the right types and amounts of food are important to keep their bodies healthy; to recognise and value cultural differences and diversity **Maths:** to use a variety of practical resources and contexts to help them develop understanding of number and solve simple problems **Science:** humans and other animals

Sustainable development

Activity 34 Into the future (Upper KS1/P3)

This activity is adapted from *Citizenship for the Future* by David Hicks.

Learning intention — For pupils to begin to understand the impact of humans on the environment, to have an awareness of the past and future, to develop an enquiring mind and a concern for the wider environment. To be aware that our actions have consequences.

Resources
- A3 paper and pencils

Activity — On their paper, ask the pupils to draw a timeline which forks in two (see diagram). On the straight part, they should note important events in their lives so far. The forked part allows events for the next 100 years to be shown. The top fork is for 'preferable futures' – this is for pupils to note things that they hope will happen in their own lives. The bottom fork is for 'probable futures', where pupils record things which they feel are likely to happen in their own lives. On completion, as a class, talk about the differences between the two 'futures'. Then discuss ways in which pupils' 'preferable futures' could be achieved.

As an additional activity, a separate timeline of global events, with preferable futures (what the pupils hope will happen in the world) and probable futures (what they think is likely to happen in the world) can also be drawn. These can then be compared with the personal timelines.

Note: *Probable global futures can sometimes be pessimistic, but comparison with and discussion about preferable futures can counter this.*

Planned outcome   For pupils to be aware of the future and begin to realise that they have a role to play in determining what that will be like.

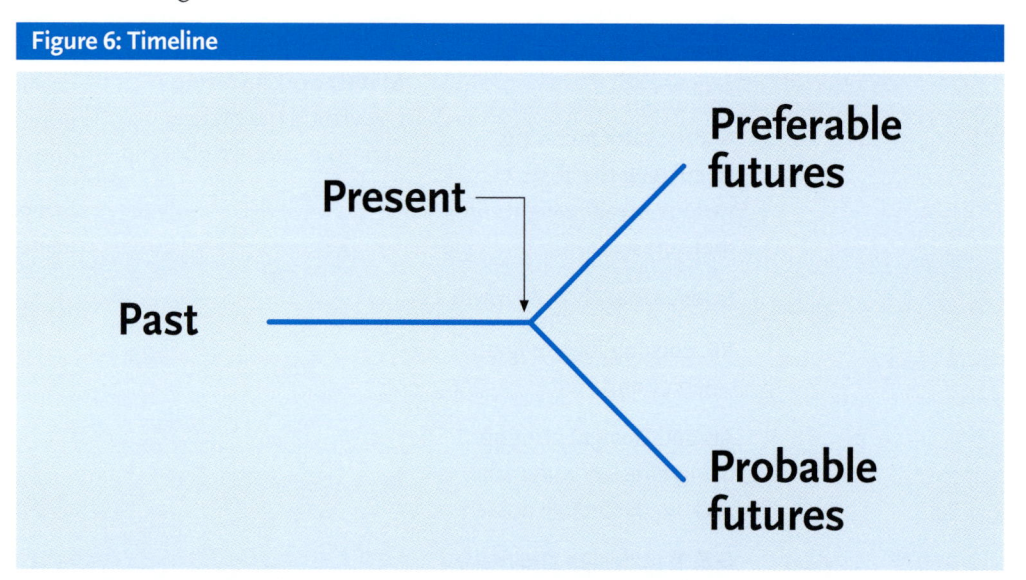

Figure 6: Timeline

Past — Present — Preferable futures / Probable futures

Curriculum links

England	Scotland	Wales
PSHE/Citizenship: for pupils to share their opinions on things that matter to them and explain their views; to recognise choices they can make; to consider simple social and moral dilemmas; to take part in discussions **Science:** ourselves **Literacy Hour:** Year 1, term 3	**PSD:** interdependence: decisions about personal, social and environmental responsibilities which will affect their own and others' present and future lifestyles **Environmental Studies/ Science:** consequences for living things and for the environment of different choices, decisions and courses of action	**PSE:** to begin to express their own views and ideas; to recognise and express their feelings **English:** to write in response to a range of stimuli, and in a range of forms

Activity 35   Sustainable living board game

This activity requires more than one session.

Learning intention   Pupils begin to develop an enquiring mind, state an opinion based on evidence, value resources and understand our impact on the environment.

Resources
- large sheets of paper or card on which to make board games
- counters and dice

information about living sustainably (see bullet points opposite)

Activity

In a whole group, ask the pupils how they can live in a sustainable way – in other words, how to live in a healthy way, respecting others and the environment. Encourage pupils to talk about how they can live more sustainably at school and at home. To give them some ideas, you could ask about ways of:

- keeping healthy – not smoking, eating a balanced diet
- respecting others – being considerate to others, looking after other people's things
- respecting the environment – saving water, electricity and paper, recycling.

Write some of the ideas on the classroom board, and show the information gathered. Ask pupils in pairs to think up about 15 pieces of text requiring players to go forward or back, such as 'Didn't turn tap off properly, go back 2' or 'Fitted energy-saving light bulbs, go on 3'. The text needs to be brief to go in particular squares on the board game. Then the pupils can draw out as creatively as possible a simple board game track of about 50 squares. Their prepared texts can then be spread out around the track. On completion, play the games in groups, taking turns so that everyone's game is played. (You might need a games slot for a couple of days to do this.) To spread the energy-saving word further, a younger or parallel class could be invited in to play the games.

Planned outcome

That pupils begin to realise that everyone can behave responsibly with regard to the world's resources, and make a difference for the good.

Curriculum links

England	Scotland	Wales
PSHE/Citizenship: to take and share responsibility; to make real choices; to consider simple environmental issues **Maths:** shape and measurement **Literacy Hour:** Year 1, term 1; Year 2, term 1	**PSD:** interdependence; decisions about personal, social and environmental responsibilities which will affect their own and others' present and future lifestyles **Environmental Studies/Science:** consequences for living things and for the environment of different choices, decisions and courses of action **Environmental Studies:** the responsible use of the natural environment in accordance with the principles of sustainability **Maths:** collecting, organising and interpreting data	**PSE:** to be concerned about their environment; to understand how their environment could be made better or worse to live in and how they can make a difference **Maths:** to understand the operations of addition and subtraction **Geography:** to communicate ideas, information and opinions; to follow directions; to use secondary sources to obtain information about places **English:** to write in a range of forms

Peace and conflict resolution

Activity 36 Why do we fight?

Adapted from *Primary Values* by Alison Montgomery and Ursula Birthistle.

Learning intention For pupils to appreciate some of the causes of conflict and to begin to develop strategies of conflict resolution; to look at different viewpoints, identify unfairness and take appropriate action; to empathise with and respond to the needs of others and to be aware that our actions have consequences.

Activity Ask the pupils to think about why children might argue over possessions, friends, sport, etc. Discuss the pupils' suggestions and ask who feels they have argued for the same reasons. Ask pupils to think about situations at home or at school that can lead to fights. Use these as scenarios for role play in small groups. Ideas could include an argument over watching television, a fight over a football or book, a family row about bedtime or going out to play, or being wrongly accused and not getting a chance to explain. After each group acts out its scene, ask for class suggestions for resolving the problem. (Note that reversing the roles is an effective way of building empathy.)

Planned outcome That pupils gain increased awareness of the causes, and possible resolution of difficulties.

Curriculum links

England	Scotland	Wales
PSHE/Citizenship: to recognise choices they can make, and the difference between right and wrong; to consider social and moral dilemmas that they come across in everyday life (e.g. aggressive behaviour); to ask for help **Literacy Hour:** Year 2, term 1	**PSD:** Interpersonal relationships; to demonstrate respect and tolerance for those whose opinions differ from their own **Environmental Studies:** conflict and decision making **English:** talking and listening	**PSE:** to begin to express their own views and ideas; to recognise and express their own feelings **Oracy:** to participate in drama activities and improvisation; to listen with growing attention and concentration so that they respond appropriately and effectively to what they have heard

Activity 37 Sunflowers

The idea for this activity is adapted from *Global Teacher, Global Learner* by Graham Pike and David Selby.

Although it only takes one session to make the sunflowers, the activity is designed to be continued over a period of time.

Learning intention For pupils to begin to state an opinion based on evidence, empathise with and respond to the needs of others, and develop an awareness of and pride in their individuality.

Resources	- coloured paper and pencils
- scissors
- glue
- pupils' photographs if desired
Activity	Each pupil makes a large paper sunflower stalk, leaves and centre without the petals. They can write their name on one of the leaves, with a photo or drawing of themselves in the middle. The incomplete sunflowers are then put on the wall, near a supply of cut-out petals. Whenever a pupil wishes to make an affirmative remark about another pupil, they write it on a petal and stick it on that person's sunflower. You can also add remarks if someone is being left out. Completed sunflowers will show affirmative remarks for each pupil.
Planned outcome	For pupils to understand that there are good things about everyone, and it is helpful to tell people so.

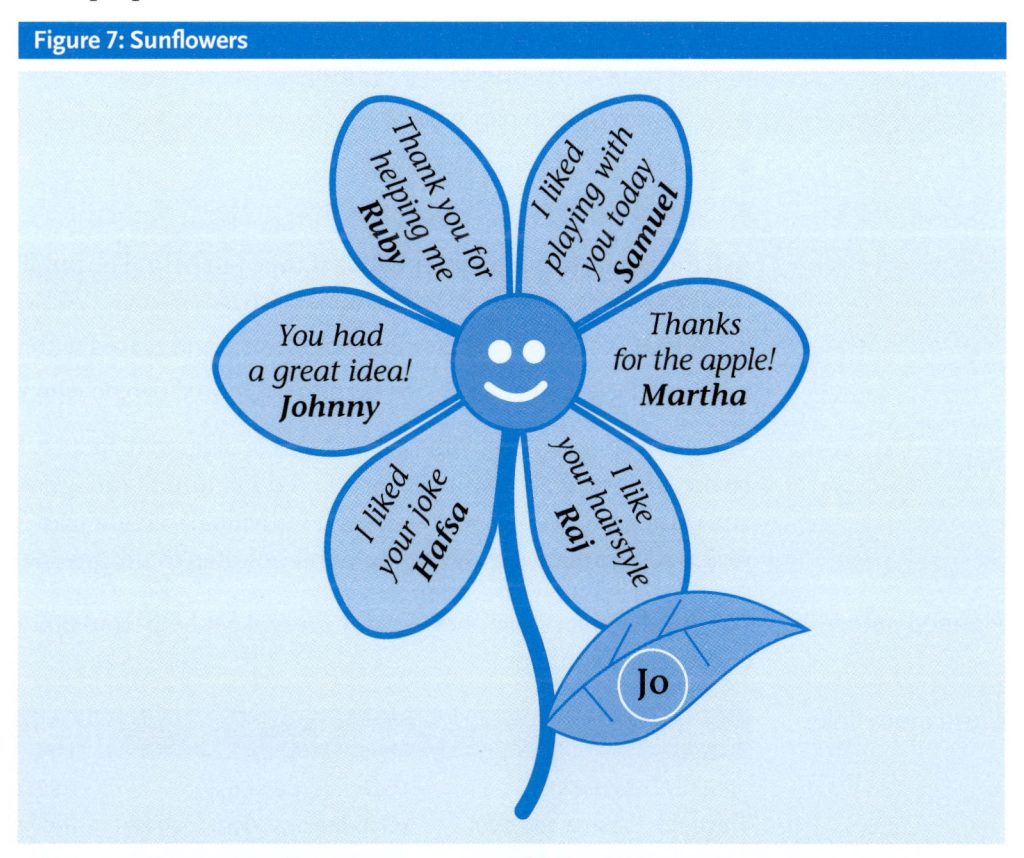

Figure 7: Sunflowers

Petals:
- Thank you for helping me **Ruby**
- I liked playing with you today **Samuel**
- You had a great idea! **Johnny**
- Thanks for the apple! **Martha**
- I liked your joke **Hafsa**
- I like your hairstyle **Raj**

Leaf: **Jo**

Curriculum links

England	Scotland	Wales
PSHE/Citizenship: to contribute to the life of the class; that friends should care for each other; to feel positive about themselves; to recognise how their behaviour affects other people **Art and Design:** self-portraits	**PSD:** positive regard for self and for others and their needs **Expressive Arts:** positive attitude to self and others **Environmental Studies:** developing informed attitudes; cultural and social diversity	**PSE:** to feel positive about themselves; to respect others and value their achievements

Activity 38   Can I help?

This is a circle time activity adapted from *Turn Your School Round* by Jenny Mosely.

Depending on how many pupils need help, this takes one or two sessions to put in place, but needs follow-up.

Note: *Although we have given an example of a circle time activity here, it is a technique which has certain conventions and we would recommend further reading on it. (See Chapter 6.)*

Learning intention   For pupils to appreciate some of the causes of conflict and to begin to develop strategies of conflict resolution; for pupils to empathise with and respond to the needs of others, to show tact and diplomacy, and a willingness to learn from the experiences of others.

Activity   Ask the pupils if anyone has a problem they would like some help with. Remind them that in circle time they cannot mention anyone's name negatively. Answers might include:

- 'I need help because I keep fighting ...'
- 'I have no one to play with ...'
- 'I don't get on with my work ...'
- 'Somebody keeps calling me names'.

Ask the pupils to put up their hands if they can help. The pupil needing help then chooses someone, who asks questions such as:

- 'Would it help if I. ...?' (for example, 'came and played with you')
- 'Would it help if you ...?' (for example, 'ignored people who you might fight with').

The pupil being advised then gives their considered response, such as 'Yes, it would be nice if I could play with you' or 'No, I don't think I can ignore them'. The pupil and class group jointly decides on the individual's action plan for the week, to be reviewed the following week. The pupil can then thank anyone who helped them.

Planned outcome   For pupils to learn that they can ask for and get help from others, and that others are concerned about them.

Curriculum links

England	Scotland	Wales
PSHE/Citizenship: to recognise, name and deal with their feelings in a positive way; to recognise choices they can make, and the difference between right and wrong; to listen to others; to feel positive about themselves; to recognise how their behaviour affects other people and that there are different types of teasing and bullying; that bullying is wrong, and how to get help	**PSD:** interpersonal relationships; demonstrate respect and tolerance for those whose opinions differ from their own **Environmental Studies:** conflict and decision making	**PSE:** to begin to express their own views and ideas; to know how to be a good friend; to understand that they can take on some responsibility in their friendship groups **Oracy:** to ask and answer questions that clarify their understanding and indicate thoughtfulness about the matter under discussion

KS2 (England and Wales), P4–P7 (Scotland)

Most of these activities will take between 40 and 60 minutes. The others, which are marked, will take a half-day or a whole day or even longer. Most can be extended into longer activities if desired. We have also noted where we feel activities are best suited to the top end of the age group. The activities here each address aspects of Global Citizenship: you can see which aspects by looking at the learning intentions at the start of each activity. (Also see mapping on pages 53–58.)

The activities will also deliver substantial aspects of the English PSHE/Citizenship Guidelines, the Welsh PSE Framework, and the Scottish 5–14 Environmental Studies, 5–14 English Language and 5–14 PSD Guidelines. Each activity also has further links with other English, Welsh and Scottish curriculum subjects. These links are shown in the table beneath each activity. Most curriculum references are relevant for Wales as well as England, and specific references to the Welsh National Curriculum are highlighted. Many of the activities also promote the National Healthy Schools Scheme in England.

A note about simulation games

Simulation games are an extremely graphic way of explaining some complex issues of Global Citizenship, especially social justice and equity, globalisation and interdependence and sustainable development. They can also show that resources can be allocated in different ways, which affect individuals, communities and the sustainability of the environment. Many are for secondary level, but there are recommendations in Chapter 6 for primary schools. Some simulation games require quite a lot of preparation – see the instructions for individual games.

Social justice and equity

Activity 39   Captions!

Learning intention   For pupils to understand the nature of prejudice and ways to combat it; to be able to detect bias, opinion and stereotypes; to assess different viewpoints and to recognise and start to challenge unfairness, and to promote a sense of justice.

Resources
- magazines and newspapers
- scissors, glue, paper
- some examples of photographs and captions that promote stereotypes, generalised or racist views, such as 'Africa is ...', 'asylum seekers are ...'

Activity   Pupils cut out five photographs from magazines or newspapers and stick them on a clean sheet of paper. Ask them to write one negative and one positive caption for each of the pictures. Display the work and discuss the impact the different captions have on our perceptions of the places and any people in the photographs. Then discuss the pictures and captions from the newspapers you have brought in. Encourage pupils to question the captions and to suggest or write more suitable ones. For example, if the captions are generalist or stereotyped, think up alternative captions which explain in which place, or among which particular group of people something has happened. If discriminatory captions are found, encourage the pupils to write a class letter to the editor of the paper outlining their concerns.

	Planned outcome	For pupils to realise that the media can be manipulative and can perpetuate stereotyped views, and that they are able to think critically.

Curriculum links

England	Scotland	Wales
PSHE/Citizenship: for pupils to talk and write about their opinions, and explain their views, on issues that affect them and society; to explore how the media present information; to recognise and challenge stereotypes **Literacy Hour:** Year 3, term 3; Year 4, term 3; Year 5, term 3; Year 6, term 2.	**PSD:** positive regard for others **Environmental Studies:** people in society; to develop an understanding of the influence of the media; to identify conflicting points of view; to develop informed attitudes; cultural and social diversity in terms of gender, race, religion, opinion or attitude	**PSE:** to recognise the importance of equality of opportunity; to understand how injustice and inequality affect people's lives **English:** *Reading* – to read texts with challenging subject matter that broadens perspectives and extends thinking *Writing* – to write in response to a range of stimuli, in forms which include non-fiction **Oracy:** to identify and comment on key features of what they see and hear in a variety of media

Activity 40   Homelessness

This could take longer than one session, depending on the debate or speakers.

Learning intention For pupils to understand the causes and effects of inequality and the impact of conflict; to develop an empathy towards others locally; to develop a belief that things can be better and that individuals can make a difference.

Resources
- information about homelessness
- *Big Issue* magazines – these will provide testimonies or accounts from homeless people

Activity Ask pupils to brainstorm words about what a home provides, and talk about as many different types of homes as possible in the UK, including caravans, castles, benders, and house-boats. Then talk about people without homes, for example, people living on the streets. Ask pupils whether they have met or seen any homeless people. Encourage pupils to find information about homelessness. For instance, provide pupils with testimonies and accounts to read about the lives of particular people, which give reasons for them being homeless. Ask pupils to research what types of shelters homeless people are able to make, and where some homeless people live. Discuss the pupils' findings in a whole-class session and jointly come up with ways of doing something positive. Ideas could include:

- finding out more about the reasons for, and issues of, homelessnesss by hearing directly from either a homeless person, or someone who works with them; in addition, enable pupils to gain views from people opposed to supporting the homeless, with their reasons
- holding a debate on a topic such as 'No-one should be homeless in the UK', using all the information gained above
- looking out for examples of biased and stereotyped views in the media and elsewhere about homeless people, and if these are found, writing letters to express their views on how homeless people should be treated.

Planned outcome That pupils will gain increased awareness of issues of homelessness, including that some people have more choice than others in this matter; that they feel empathy towards people in difficult situations and are willing to do something positive to help.

Curriculum links

England	Scotland	Wales
PSHE/Citizenship: to talk about their opinions, and explain their views, on issues that effect themselves and society; to reflect on spiritual, moral, social and cultural issues, using imagination to understand other people's experiences; to think about the lives of people living in other places **D & T:** shelters **Science:** characteristics of materials **ICT:** analysing data and asking questions	**PSD:** positive regard for others **Environmental Studies:** to develop an understanding of individual and social needs, rights and responsibilities	**PSE:** to show care and consideration for others and to be sensitive towards their feelings **Oracy:** to explore, develop and explain ideas; to make a range of contributions in discussions

Activity 41   What is a global citizen? (Upper KS2/ P4)

Learning intention For pupils to realise their potential to change things; to accept and act on group decisions, to compromise; to gain a sense of importance and self-worth and a growing respect for difference and diversity; to hold a belief that things can be better and that individuals can make a difference.

Resources A set of the nine points listed below, per group of about four or five. Each point needs to be on a separate slip of paper.

1 I try to understand how other people are feeling.
2 I am as important as everyone else.
3 Everyone else is equal to me but different from me.
4 I know what is fair and not fair and try to do the right thing.
5 I look after the environment and don't waste things.
6 I try to help others and not fight with them.

7 I have my own ideas but can alter them if I realise they are wrong.

8 I want to learn more about the world.

9 I think I can change things in the world.

Activity

In small discussion groups, ask pupils to place the statements in order of importance. This can be done in the form of a diamond with the most important statement at the top and the least important at the bottom. Statements of equal importance are placed alongside each other – see diagram.

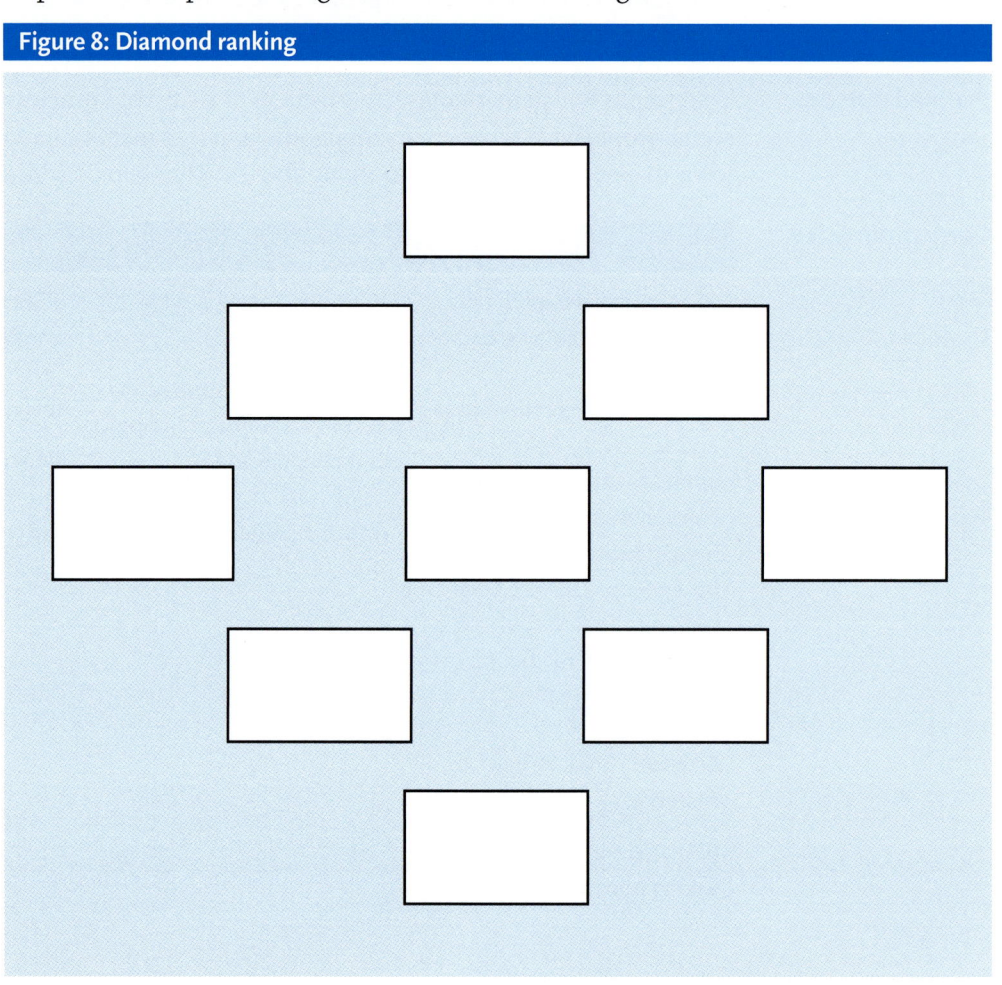

Figure 8: Diamond ranking

Pupils need to work cooperatively and to give reasons to others within their group for their individual views. After about 15 minutes discuss the activity as a whole class, with each group explaining what their final layout was, and why. Then ask the pupils to work in groups on what they could do to show that these things are important. For instance, under the first point, suggestions might include listening to others, asking others what is wrong or how they are feeling, or befriending others who are lonely. The most difficult one for the pupils to do is probably, 'I am as important as everyone else', so perhaps you could give them some examples, such as 'I am especially good at ...', or 'I help in the class by ...'. The suggestions can be written as pledges of what pupils will try to do to show they can be Global Citizens, and they can be put on display.

Planned outcome

That pupils' self-esteem is raised and they feel important, valued and able to take responsibility and change things.

Curriculum links

England	Scotland	Wales
PSHE/Citizenship: to talk and write about their opinions and explain their views; to recognise their worth as individuals; to resolve differences, make decisions and explain choices; to care about other people's feelings and try to see things from their point of view **Literacy Hour:** Year 4, term 3; Year 6, term 2	**PSD:** tolerance and respect **Environmental Studies:** to develop an understanding of the concept of equity in a fair and caring multicultural society **English:** talking about feelings and experiences	**PSE:** to feel positive about themselves and be confident in their own values; to express their views and ideas confidently and take part in a debate **Oracy:** to share ideas, insights and opinions, make a range of contributions in discussions, and listen to others, questioning them to clarify what they mean and extending or following up the ideas

Globalisation and interdependence

Activity 42   Our links around the world

Learning intention For pupils to appreciate the contribution of different cultures, values and beliefs to their lives, to begin to understand trade between countries, and to have a growing interest in world events.

Resources
- an A4 copy of the table 'Our links around the world' (Worksheet 11) for each pair of children
- pencils
- a globe or map

Activity Give each pair a copy of the table. Ask the pupils to discuss each question and add their answers. In every case, there is more than one answer.

In a whole class session, share and discuss the answers. This gives you a chance to challenge stereotypes and to move pupils' thinking onwards: a language spoken in the UK could of course be Welsh, Irish, Scots or English, but could equally be any of the hundreds of other languages spoken here. Similarly, there are a huge number of places where rice is eaten in the world, including the UK. This work could be followed up by different pupils finding out more about one of the questions, for example, a charity which works overseas, or a country they have heard about, and sharing that with the class.

Another version of this kind of activity, referred to as 'Globingo', involves the pupils moving round the room and finding people who can give an answer – their name is then written in the box.

Planned outcome That pupils become aware of some of the many links between countries, and that these crop up in their daily lives.

Curriculum links

England	Scotland	Wales
PSHE/Citizenship: to recognise the role of pressure groups; to recognise and challenge stereotypes **Geography:** passport to the world – learning about different places	**PSD:** tolerance and respect **Environmental Studies:** developing informed attitudes; interdependence in a local and global context; people and places	**PSE:** to enable pupils to value and celebrate cultural difference and diversity **Geography:** places – understand and realise the interrelationships within the wider world in terms of decision making and Global Citizenship

Worksheet 11

'Think of...'

A fruit or vegetable that was grown in the UK	A language spoken in the UK	Something that comes from the rainforest of Brazil
A pressure group or charity which works overseas	A country where rice is eaten	Something you know about a country in Asia
Something you are wearing that was not made in the UK	A country you have read about or heard about	A famous person from a country in Africa

Activity 43   Fair Trade (Upper KS2/P4)

Learning intention For pupils to begin to understand trade and Fair Trade between countries, to realise their potential to change things, to begin to present a reasoned case, to recognise and start to challenge unfairness, to recognise choices and recognise their consequences, and to hold a belief that things can be better and that individuals can make a difference.

Resources
- information on the Fairtrade Foundation and catalogues of fairly traded products such as Traidcraft
- a packet to show the Fairtrade Foundation symbol
- a few examples of produce endorsed by the Fairtrade Foundation and non-Fair Trade produce for pupils to taste, such as chocolate, bananas, fruit juice
- a world map (Peters' projection, preferably – see Chapter 5, page 159)

Note: *There are only a limited number of products which are endorsed by the Fairtrade Foundation, and which carry the Fairtrade symbol of two interlocking Fs. These products include tea, coffee, sugar, bananas, snacks and biscuits, honey, chocolate and fruit juice. However, many other products sold through organisations such as Traidcraft and Oxfam are fairly traded.*

Figure 9: Fairtrade symbol

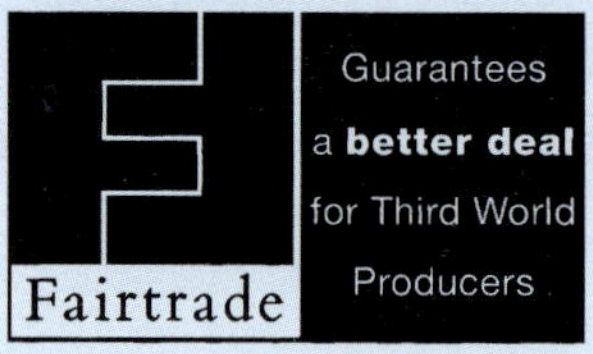

Fairtrade — Guarantees a **better deal** for Third World Producers

Activity Show the pupils the packet of a product endorsed by the Fairtrade Foundation, and describe the principles of Fair Trade. (There will probably be an explanatory message on the packaging from the manufacturer – or you can find one in materials from the Fairtrade Foundation.) The principles include:

- a guaranteed minimum price for produce
- recognised trade unions
- no child labour
- decent working conditions
- fair wages
- environmental sustainability.

Ask the pupils why they think the manufacturers are interested in having the approval of the Fairtrade Foundation.

Take the pupils to a local shop or supermarket. Ask them to choose five items including, if available, at least one Fairtrade Foundation item. For each item ask pupils to record the following information: what the item is; where it is from; who the manufacturer is; and whether or not it is a Fairtrade product. The aim is not for the pupils to buy the items! On return to the classroom, help pupils plot the items on a world map. Then discuss which countries from this sample export most things and which least, and which manufacturers produce most items. Also raise the issue of transportation of the items – the 'food miles' that long journeys from source to sale put on the goods, and the associated pollution caused by this transportation.

Focus on fairly traded products. Discuss the pros and cons (price, distance some goods have travelled as compared with locally grown food) of fairly traded goods. Give pupils the opportunity to taste and compare foods, such as Fairtrade and non-Fair Trade chocolate, bananas, fruit juice. Provide the pupils with catalogues of fairly traded goods showing a range of items. Ask pupils to access the web sites of producers of fairly traded goods and make information posters about them and their products. Encourage pupils to write letters of support or concern about Fair Trade provision to the managing director of the shop they visited. Their arguments should be presented clearly with reasons given for their interest in this issue.

Planned outcome That pupils begin to understand issues of trade and Fair Trade and that they are in a position to make informed decisions as consumers; that they can make their opinions known to people in positions where they are able to change things.

Curriculum links

England	Scotland	Wales
PSHE/Citizenship: to talk and write about their opinions, and explain their views, on issues that affect themselves and society; to face new challenges positively by collecting information, looking for help, making responsible choices, and taking action. to think about the lives of people living in other places; to take responsibility; to make real choices and informed decisions; to take part in simple debates about topical issues; to consider simple social and moral dilemmas **Geography:** Fair Trade can be brought into discussions on trade **Literacy Hour:** Year 4, term 3; Year 5, term 3; Year 6, term 2 **ICT:** analysing data and asking questions	**PSD:** to take increasing responsibility for their own lives **Environmental Studies:** to develop understanding of the importance of active citizenship, individual and social needs and relationship to economic factors; justice and equity	**PSE:** understanding the limitations on, and costs and benefits of, spending choices **Geography:** places – understand and realise the interrelationships within the wider world in terms of decision making and Global Citizenship **Oracy:** making reasoned, evaluative comments; identifying and commenting on key features of what they see and hear in a variety of media

Activity 44   *Bagchal* (Movement of the tiger)

Bagchal is an ancient board game from Nepal, requiring strategic thinking.

This activity requires more than one session.

Learning intention For pupils to value the contribution of different cultures, values and beliefs to our lives and to make choices and recognise their consequences; to have a growing respect for difference and diversity.

Resources
- *Bagchal* board, four tiger counters and 20 goat counters (you could use two different coloured counters)

Activity This is a game for two players. Player A controls the tigers and player B controls the goats. The aim of the game is for the goats to block the tigers and prevent them from moving. The tigers can jump over and thus capture a goat if the intersection immediately behind the goat is empty. Player A places the four tiger counters on the four corners of the board. Player B places one goat on any intersection on the board. Player A moves one of the tigers along any line to the next intersection aiming to capture a goat. Player B places a second goat on the board. Player A takes another turn, moving any tiger to another intersection. This continues until all the goats have been placed on the board. Player B can then move any goat along any line to the next intersection, continuing their attempt to prevent the tigers moving. The tigers cannot be captured and removed from the board. The game is over when all four tigers have been blocked or when six goats have been captured.

Photo 3: Children playing Bagchal (by Eilish Commins)

Figure 10: Bagchal board

बाग्चह

Planned outcome That pupils appreciate that there are similar games throughout the world and that skill is required to win the game.

Curriculum links

England	Scotland	Wales
PSHE/Citizenship: to think about how rules are needed in some situations; to develop relationships through work and play **Maths:** shape and measurement **Geography:** passport to the world – links with countries around the world **Literacy:** Year 4, term 1	**PSD:** interpersonal relationships **Environmental Studies:** developing informed attitudes – cultural and social diversity	**PSE:** to be honest and fair and have respect for rules, the law and authority **Maths:** shape, space and measures; to extend their understanding of position and movement **Geography:** to further their awareness of the wider world

Appreciation of diversity

Activity 45   Exploring stereotypes

Learning intention For pupils to understand the nature of prejudice and ways of combating it, to detect bias and stereotypes, and to recognise and start to challenge unfairness.

Resources
- one photograph for each pupil – ideally you would have two or more identical photos of each person, given to different pupils; you will need to use pictures of people you know something about, either cuttings from magazines or photographs of your friends!

Note: *You may need to familiarise pupils with the genre of biographies before undertaking this activity.*

Activity Discuss the meaning of 'stereotype' with the class. Give out the photos and ask pupils to write a 'biography' of their person, based on what they can infer from the photograph. In a plenary session, ask pupils to show their pictures and share their descriptions, giving reasons for their views. If identical photographs have been written about, ask pupils to read out the descriptions of these one after the other. Discuss the differences. Then tell them what you know about the person. How different is this from the pupil's comments?

Talk about what the pupils have learnt from this, and ask for their ideas as to ways of avoiding stereotyping people – for example, don't assume things about people, don't generalise, don't believe all you hear, find things out at first hand wherever possible.

Planned outcome That pupils begin to understand that you cannot make accurate judgements through assumptions, and that stereotyping can lead to unfounded prejudice.

Curriculum links

England	Scotland	Wales
PSHE/Citizenship: to appreciate the range of national, regional, religious and ethnic identities in the UK; to recognise and challenge stereotypes; that differences and similarities between people arise from a number of factors, including cultural, ethnic, racial and religious diversity, gender and disability **Literacy Hour:** Year 6, term 1 **ICT:** writing for different audiences	**PSD:** to reflect on own attitudes towards others **Environmental Studies:** developing informed attitudes; cultural and social diversity in terms of gender, colour, race, religious opinion or attitude	**PSE:** to value and celebrate cultural difference and diversity; to recognise the uniqueness and independence of individuals **Writing:** to write in response to a wide range of stimuli, use the characteristics of different kinds of writing, reflect on their use of language

Activity 46 Where is this place?

This activity is adapted from *Speaking for Ourselves, Listening to Others* published by Leeds Development Education Centre.

Learning intention For pupils to gain an awareness of the nature of prejudice and ways to combat it, be able to detect bias, opinion and stereotypes, and feel empathy towards others locally and globally.

Resources
- a copy of the statements A to D (Worksheet 12) on separate slips of paper – you will need enough for each pupil to have one statement
- some photographs and information about a country you have chosen, preferably one most pupils do not know much about

Activity In a whole-class session, ask pupils to describe the country you have chosen. Discuss where they got their information, and if they think it is true. (Ensure you counter negative stereotypes if they arise.) Tell the pupils some interesting facts about the country and show a range of photographs. Discuss how the initial views and the reality may differ.

Give out two different sets of statements from A, B, C and D to each pair of pupils.

First ask each pupil individually to decide which country is being described on their paper, giving reasons for their decision. They swap statements with their partner, and come up with a suggested country and reasons for their decision for this statement. Then they join with their partner and compare answers and reasons.

In a plenary session, ask pupils to share their thoughts. When each group has been heard, tell them that all the phrases represented views of England (use Britain if you prefer). They came from Kenyan girls (A) and boys (C) and Greek boys (B) and girls (D). Is anyone surprised? Why? Stick the statements onto a chart with two columns: those that they think do, and those that they think don't describe England. Talk about where the views may have come from – for example, the media, films, tourists, and school textbooks.

Planned outcome That pupils begin to appreciate that misconceptions about others occur throughout the world; that they begin to understand the importance of questioning information and stereotyped views.

Possible extension work Ask the pupils, working in pairs, to think about how they would portray their locality using 8–10 photographs and descriptions, to give an accurate picture of it to someone living elsewhere. Would they include a run-down area? A homeless person sleeping rough? A stately home? What are the reasons for their decisions? If possible, enable them to take digital or conventional photographs of some of the areas they feel they should include. Use these to make up a Locality Book, either computer or paper based. These could be swapped with a partner school either within or outside Britain via email or post.

Curriculum links

England	Scotland	Wales
PSHE/Citizenship: to think about the lives of people living in other places; to recognise and challenge stereotypes	**PSD:** to identify, review and evaluate the values they and society hold and recognise that these affect thoughts and actions	**PSE:** to express their views and ideas confidentially and take part in a debate; to value and celebrate cultural difference and diversity
Geography: passport to the world – learning about different places	**Environmental Studies:** people and place; developing informed attitudes	**Geography:** places – to understand and realise the interrelationships within the wider world in terms of decision making and Global Citizenship
Literacy Hour: Year 6, term 1	**English:** talking about opinions	
ICT: information about the school's locality could be put on a school website		**Oracy:** to listen and respond to a range of people; to qualify or justify what they think after listening to other opinions

Worksheet 12

A
- They eat frogs and snakes.
- There are no pickpockets.
- There are no black people.
- Guns come from there.

B
- There are big forests.
- They have large roads.
- They have beautiful coins.
- They have very tall mountains.

C
- Their policemen wear red and black uniforms.
- They live in flats.
- There are many factories.
- There are lots of churches and hospitals.

D
- There are lots of old things.
- They have a nice climate.
- There are many shops.
- It has a large population.
- The people speak a beautiful language.

© Chris Kington Publishing and Oxfam GB 2002

Activity 47   Raising awareness of disability

This activity will take more than one session.

Learning intention   For pupils to recognise the nature of prejudice and ways to combat it, to understand their potential to change things, to feel empathy towards others locally, and to have a growing respect for difference and diversity.

Resources
- information on disability, for example from the RNIB, National Deaf Children's Society, or a mobility–disability organisation
- maps or plans of the school buildings and grounds

Activity   Use a number of sources to gain information about issues of disability. These can include the pupils' own knowledge, materials from organisations concerned with disability, Radio 4's *In Touch* programme or BBC 2's *See Hear* programme, and visitors. Promote discussion and challenge stereotypes about disabled people and the issues faced by disabled people on a daily basis. In groups, ask the pupils to tour the school buildings and grounds, bearing in mind how accessible they are for particular disabled people: those who are visually, hearing or mobility impaired. Annotate plans of the school showing:

- areas which are well designed for people with particular impairments (note which impairments); good design could include induction loops in the hall for hearing impaired people, coloured edges to paving and steps, ramps, handrails and appropriate toilets
- areas which are badly designed, such as steps, poor disabled access, narrow passages
- additional barriers to disabled people, such as bags of rubbish, uneven paving, potholes.

In a plenary session, compare the plans, discuss what has arisen and decide how far the class or school can go to improve things for disabled people within the school. Implement these ideas if possible. (This might require community help.) If possible, do a similar survey to the one above in a local road. Discuss ways pupils can be more mindful of these issues in their everyday lives. Ideas include not leaving bicycles lying across the pavement, and not dropping litter that someone could slip on in the street.

Planned outcome   That pupils are enabled to become more aware of issues of disability, and realise that considering issues for disabled people leads to improving the environment for everyone, and that disabled people have the same rights as everyone else; an appreciation that most disabled people have good ideas, a job and a sense of humour just like most non-disabled people.

Curriculum links

England	Scotland	Wales
PSHE/Citizenship: that there are different kinds of responsibilities in the community; to reflect on social issues, using imagination to understand other people's experiences; to take responsibility for the needs of others **Geography:** making maps and plans **Literacy Hour:** Year 6, term 2 **ICT:** graphic modelling, analysing data and asking question	**PSD:** interpersonal relationships **Environmental Studies:** developing informed attitudes – concepts of justice and equality of opportunity for all	**PSE:** to recognise the importance of equality of opportunity; to work cooperatively to tackle problems **Geography:** to collect, record and present evidence to answer questions; to observe, collect and record information in the field **Reading:** to find information in books and ICT-based sources; to read and use a wide range of sources of information

Sustainable development

Activity 48   Welcome to the puppet show!

This activity will take more than one session.

Learning intention   **For pupils to realise their potential to change things; to find and select evidence; to make and recognise the consequences of choices; to compromise; to develop a sense of importance of individual worth and a belief that things can be better and that individuals can make a difference.**

Resources
- paper, card and crayons/paints
- scissors, glue and collage materials
- one large cardboard box per group

Activity   Role-play yourself, or brief a small group of children to role-play some unhealthy behaviour, such as eating crisps for breakfast, smoking, or insisting on going everywhere in the car. Discuss these scenarios. Then brainstorm ideas for what constitutes a healthy lifestyle including, for example, exercise, healthy eating, hygiene routines, reducing risky behaviour, road safety, not taking drugs. Provide the pupils with information and internet access, and ask them in groups of about four or five to find out as much as possible about one of the ideas.

In a plenary session, share the pupils' findings and discuss the issues. Ask each group to devise a puppet play based on their research, to teach younger pupils about healthy lifestyles. They will need to write the play script, make the characters, and find or make props. Make one theatre set from a large cardboard box, suitably decorated (or each group can do their own if there is time). Ensure that you know the content of all the plays, and raise issues with particular groups where necessary.

Allow each group to perform its play to the class, and to receive positive feedback. Then decide on the best way of performing to the other classes in the school, either by inviting other classes to your class, or by sending pupils to perform in other classes.

Planned outcome That pupils gain knowledge about different aspects of healthy lifestyles, that they appreciate the responsibility for their lifestyle rests increasingly with them, and that they are concerned to pass on sensible information to younger pupils.

Curriculum links

England	Scotland	Wales
PSHE/Citizenship: covers a number of the 'Developing a healthy, safer lifestyle' guidelines, depending on the content, e.g. the benefits of exercise, healthy eating, hygiene routines, reducing risky behaviour, road safety, not taking drugs, what affects mental health, how to make informed choices, and first aid; pressure to behave in an unacceptable way can come from a variety of sources, including people they know; how to ask for help and use basic techniques for resisting pressure to do wrong; National Healthy Schools Standard **Science:** teeth and eating, keeping healthy **Literacy Hour:** Year 3, term 1; Year 4, term 1; Year 5, term 1	**PSD:** interpersonal relationships **Environmental Studies:** health – taking responsibility for health; developing informed attitudes – rights and responsibilities in society **English Language:** imaginative writing, sense of audience	**PSE:** to understand the benefits of exercise and hygiene; to express their views and ideas confidently **Science:** humans and other animals – nutrition, circulation, movement, health **English:** *Reading* – to find information in books and ICT-based sources, to read and use a wide range of sources of information *Oracy* – to participate in a wide range of drama activities including the writing and performance of scripted drama

Activity 49   Sustainable living sourcebook (Upper KS2/ P6)

This activity could continue over several sessions.

Learning intention For pupils to begin to understand the relationship between people and the environment, to be aware of finite resources, to present a reasoned case, and to feel a sense of responsibility for the environment and the use of resources

Resources
- definitions of sustainable development (see Chapter 2 page 28, Worksheet 8)
- some information on ideas for sustainable living (more can be gathered as part of the work)
- paper and crayons
- scissors and glue

Activity As a class, look at some definitions of sustainable development. Discuss the meaning and implications of this for humankind and more specifically for each individual in the class.

Discuss the idea of producing a class 'sustainable living sourcebook' – a resource full of ideas and information about how we can live more sustainability. On completion, it could be exchanged with a school elsewhere to compare local approaches to sustainable living.

Divide the class into three. Give each third responsibility to find out about how we can live more sustainably in one of the following situations:

- at home
- at school
- in the local community.

Here are some ideas that could be explored.

At home and at school:

- ways of saving resources such as paper, electricity, water
- ways of promoting healthy eating
- ways of reducing waste, such as buying snacks with less packaging on them, composting fruit and vegetable remains
- ways of reusing and recycling materials, containers, toys, books – for example, washing out and decorating used tins for plant pots, storage containers or sculptures, taking unwanted saleable items to charity shops or jumble sales
- ways of travelling to school which use few resources.

At home:

- ways of buying less – use the library and video hire shop instead of buying too many books or videos, mend things, and make things.

At school:

- information about the present biodiversity of the school habitat, and how it could be increased
- information about the sustainable development policy of the school, or if there is not one in place, ideas for what could go into one
- information about a local scrap project for the provision of art materials.

In the community:

- information about the practices of local businesses on sustainable development issues such as Fair Trade, use of tropical hardwoods or recycling
- ways of stating opinion about and raising public awareness of local issues such as the local environment, road-building or house-building schemes, provision of green areas, recycling
- information about local sustainable development initiatives
- information about sustainable forms of energy such as solar and wind power.

This information can be gathered by pupils in a variety of ways – for example, from books, websites, newspaper or magazine articles, or by pupils sending emails or faxing questions to relevant organisations, individuals or businesses. Try introducing the topic by inviting a local expert, such as the Local Agenda 21 officer or someone from the local Development Education Centre or an environmental group.

The sourcebook could be electronic, with information and images from websites, printed or imported into a DTP or word-processing package, graphs or pie charts included, and photographs added using a digital camera. Alternatively, the sourcebook could be in the form of a scrapbook, with information printed out from web sites, articles written on computer or by hand, and drawings being cut and pasted into it.

The finished sourcebook could be exchanged (electronically or by post) with another school or be displayed locally, perhaps at the local library or Local Education Authority or Local Agenda 21 office. Encourage the local paper or radio station to report the venture and to interview representatives of the class about their ideas and concerns.

Planned outcome For pupils to feel committed to sustainable development, to see it as relevant to them, and to learn that they can make act to make a difference.

Curriculum links

England	Scotland	Wales
PSHE/Citizenship: resources can be allocated in different ways which affect individuals, communities and the sustainability of the environment; to feel positive about themselves and their achievements; to make real choices and decisions; to develop relationships through work; to research, discuss and debate topical issues and problems; to consider social and moral dilemmas; to find information **Maths:** graphs and charts **Geography:** improving the environment **ICT:** analysing data and asking questions; graphical modelling; evaluating information **Literacy Hour:** Year 4, term 1; Year 6, term 1 **Science:** habitats	**PSD:** independence and interdependence **Environmental Studies:** developing an understanding of the interaction between people and the Earth's natural environment: land use, resources and change, environmental issues and sustainability; developing informed attitudes; social and environmental responsibility	**PSE:** to take increasing responsibility for their actions; to take an active interest in the life of the community and be concerned about the wider environment; to know how the environment can be affected by human activity **Maths:** to collect and represent discrete data using appropriate graphs and diagrams **Geography:** to investigate ways in which people attempt to look after the environment through sustainable development; to understand the individual's responsibility for the environment **English:** *Reading* – to find information in books and ICT-based sources; to read and use a wide range of sources of information *Writing* – to write in response to more demanding tasks and a wider range of purposes

Activity 50   Working children

Learning intention   For pupils to begin to understand the causes and effects of inequality, to understand trade between countries, Fair Trade, and our potential to change things; to recognise the consequences of choices.

Resources
- information on working children in the UK and abroad, in addition if possible to the statements below
- information on child labour and on initiatives to address it, for example from RUGMARK UK, a charity focused on the production and kitemarking of carpets (see Chapter 6)

Activity   Talk about what kinds of jobs children in the class do for their parents or for others. Do they get paid? Should they get paid? Then present the following information about working children by telling each as a story, or through role play. Ask them where they think these things happened (UNICEF, *The State of the World's Children*).

1. A 12-year-old was paid £5 for working 3 days in a clothing factory. (UK)
2. A 13-year-old washes vegetables in a market from 8 am until 10 pm, earning £12.50 a month. (India)
3. A 14-year-old boy was killed when he was knocked off his bicycle when delivering papers. (UK)
4. Girls aged 12 and 13 were locked in a factory where the temperature reached 37 degrees centigrade and there was no drinking water. (Honduras, in a US-based transnational company)

Look at the information on issues of working children. As a class, discuss working children. Include the reasons for children wanting or having to work, what jobs they might be able to do, if and what they should be paid, and what difficulties working children might face. Are there any circumstances in which children should not be working?

Divide the class in half and ask pupils to make notes either for or against children working, with a view to holding a class debate on the pros and cons of children working. To widen the debate, two classes in the same school could debate the issue, or another school could be involved either face to face or electronically through videoconferencing or a chat-room.

Finally, a code for working children could be devised by the pupils. Compare this with the principles laid down by organisations such as RUGMARK. Discuss this type of marking and its benefits.

Planned outcome   That pupils are enabled to think about issues of child labour here and overseas, and gain an understanding of initiatives addressing the issue.

Curriculum links

England	Scotland	Wales
PSHE/Citizenship: to reflect on moral and social issues, using imagination to understand other people's experiences; to think about the lives of people living in other places; to consider social and moral dilemmas that they come across in life **Literacy Hour:** Year 4, term 3; Year 5, term 3; Year 6, term 2	**PSD:** Interpersonal relationships **Environmental Studies:** developing an understanding of individual and social needs and the relationship to economic factors; developing informed attitudes/concepts of justice and equality of opportunity for all	**PSE:** know that people differ in what they believe is right and wrong; show care and consideration for others and be sensitive towards their feelings; empathise with others experiences and feelings **Oracy:** make a range of contributions on discussions; listen carefully, recall and re-present important features of an argument

Peace and conflict resolution

Activity 51 Investigating democracy (Upper KS2/ P6)

Learning intention For pupils to assess different viewpoints, begin to present a reasoned case, develop a sense of importance and individual worth, and hold a belief that things can be better and that individuals can make a difference.

Resources
- slips of paper and pencils
- a hat or box to put slips in

Activity Discuss the meaning of 'democracy' with the class, how it is supported within the country and how it allows people to take part in making and changing rules. Ask them to name some democracies around the world, such as India, France, South Africa. Discuss why democracies are fairer than other systems of government. Look at democracy in the pupil's own lives, and ask them in groups or pairs to write down several statements on different pieces of paper about fairness and rights within a democracy. For instance, children should be able to wear what they like to school; everyone should vote who is eligible to do so; people should be able to say anything they want in public or in the media in a democracy; children should be able to vote. In a plenary session, ask the pupils to put their ideas into a hat, which you pull out to read one at a time. If they agree with the statement, the pupils stand with their hands up, if they are not sure they stand with hands down, and if they disagree they sit down. Ask a couple of those in each pose for their reasons every time.

Planned outcome That pupils begin to understand the meaning of democracy, appreciate how it can work in their everyday lives, and are encouraged to formulate reasoned opinions.

Curriculum links

England	Scotland	Wales
PSHE/Citizenship: how to take part in making and changing rules; that there are different kinds of responsibilities, rights and duties at home, at school and in the community, and that these can sometimes conflict with each other; what democracy is, and about the basic institutions that support it locally and nationally; to consider social and moral dilemmas **History:** ancient Greece **Literacy Hour:** Year 6, term 2	**PSD:** interpersonal relationships **Environmental Studies:** developing an understanding of individual and collective rights and responsibilities in a democratic society; developing informed attitudes/concepts of justice and equality of opportunity for all	**PSE:** to be honest and fair and have respect for rules, the law and authority; to understand the importance of democratic decision making and involvement **Oracy:** to talk for a range of purposes; to listen and respond to a range of people

Activity 52 Peace and conflict in the news (Upper KS2/ P6)

This activity could continue over several weeks.

Learning intention For pupils to begin to understand some causes of conflict and some strategies for tackling conflict and for conflict prevention; to be able to detect bias, opinion and stereotypes; to find and select evidence; to have a growing interest in world events.

Resources
- a selection of newspapers, both tabloid and broadsheet, for the duration of the activity

Activity Ask the pupils to keep a corridor display board diary of peace and conflict news items for the benefit of the whole school. Include local and international events, initially by finding reports in the newspapers you have brought in. Then encourage pupils to bring articles in from home, write up things they have heard from television or radio, or download articles from news web sites. Both successful conflict resolutions and continuing disputes should be included. It is important that reports are taken from different types of papers, and for pupils to look for media bias in, for instance comparing two reports of the same event. The pupils could take it in turns to change the news and manage the display over the duration of the activity. If this activity is set to run for the term, appoint a committee with an editor. Encourage the whole school to become involved, with representatives from different classes, the office, the lunch-time supervisors and others bringing items in for the board. (Ties in with Local and Global News, see Assemblies, page 47.)

Planned outcome That pupils increase their awareness and understanding of current events, local and global, as well as media presentation of information, and that they take on the responsibility for maintaining an interesting and informative display for the benefit of the whole school.

Curriculum links

England	Scotland	Wales
PSHE/Citizenship: to realise the nature and consequences of antisocial and aggressive behaviours, such as bullying and racism, on individuals and communities; to take responsibility; to participate; to explore how the media present information; to find information **Literacy Hour:** Year 4, term 1; Year 4, term 3; Year 6, term 1 **ICT:** analysing data and asking questions; evaluating information, checking accuracy and questioning plausibility	**PSD:** interpersonal relationships **Environmental Studies:** ability to act in ways that are sensitive to global and development issues; understanding of conflict and decision-making processes, including the influence of the media **ICT:** to be aware of the implications and appreciate the need for responsible use of ICT	**PSE:** to understand how conflict can arise from different views about environmental issues; to know that people differ in what they believe to be right and wrong **Reading:** to read texts with challenging subject matter; to use inference, deduction and prediction to evaluate the texts they read; to pose pertinent questions about a topic they are investigating

References

Burningham, John (1993) *Aldo*, Red Fox.

Bliss, T., Robinson, G. and Maines, B. (1995) *Developing Circle Time*, Lucky Duck Publishing.

Dickens, Charles (1994) *A Christmas Carol*, Ladybird Books.

Foreman, Michael (1987) *Panda's Puzzle and His Voyage of Discovery*, Puffin Books.

Foreman, Michael (1999) *Dinosaurs and all that Rubbish*, Longman.

Fountain, Susan (1994) *Learning Together: Global Education 4–7*, WWF-UK.

Garlake, Teresa (2001) *Your World, My World*, Oxfam.

Harrison, Jean (1999) *Shompa Lives in India*, Christian Aid.

Hicks, David (2000) *Citizenship for the Future: A practical classroom guide*, WWF-UK.

Hollyer, Beatrice (1999) *Wake up, World!*, Frances Lincoln in association with Oxfam.

MacLellan, Gordon (1995) *Talking to the Earth*, Capall Bann Publishing.

Montgomery, Alison and Birthistle, Ursula (2001) *Primary Values*, CCEA.

Mosely, Jenny (1993) *Turn Your School Round*, LDA.

Pike, Graham and Selby, David (1988) *Global Teacher, Global Learner*, Hodder & Stoughton.

Ritson, Chrys (1996) *Speaking for Ourselves, Listening to Others*, Leeds DEC.

Sandbach, Trish and Fensome, Jo (1995) *Feeling Good About Faraway Friends*, Leeds DEC.

'The Two Mules' from *Quaker Peace & Social Witness* (see Chapter 6, page 182). This image appears on the cover of Tom Leimdorfer (1992) *Once Upon a Conflict*, Quaker Communications Department of the Religious Society of Friends.

UNICEF *The State of the World's Children* (published annually).

Wilde, Oscar (1982) *The Selfish Giant*, Puffin Books.

Chapter 4
Global Citizenship and Literacy

This series of lessons shows how issues of Global Citizenship can be incorporated into Literacy. Good-quality texts have been chosen to provide thought-provoking material that will generate interest and discussion. The lessons have been written to develop understanding and awareness of Global Citizenship issues while also providing progression in Literacy skills.

For those teachers following the Literacy Strategy, the lessons are designed to fit in with Year 2, Year 4 and Year 6. The objectives covered in the Literacy Strategy are highlighted at the beginning of each series of lessons. The lessons are equally suitable for English/Literacy lessons in Scotland and Wales.

Emphasis has been given to comprehension and composition (text-level work), with grammar and punctuation (sentence-level work) and spelling and vocabulary (word-level work) being incorporated where the links are appropriate. It is anticipated that other aspects of sentence-level and word-level work will be covered separately. The materials lend themselves well to the development of speaking and listening skills.

The work has been differentiated, but teachers may need to extend this further to suit the needs of the pupils.

The length of each series of lessons is flexible. There is much scope for extending them further, to allow deeper discussions of the issues. Ways of investigating the issues further include circle time activities, assembly preparation and presentation, and role play.

The worksheets at the end of each series of lessons, to be used as whole-class texts, can be photocopied for use on an overhead projector or enlarged on a photocopier for the class to read.

Bullying

This series of lessons is suitable for use in Year 2 and Year 3. If you are following the Literacy Strategy, it is particularly designed to fit in with Year 2, term 1.

Learning objectives

The following objectives are covered in this series of lessons.

Comprehension and composition (text-level work)

- T. 4 To understand time and sequential relationships in stories – what happened when.
- T. 5 To identify and discuss reasons for events in stories, linked to plot.
- T. 6 To discuss familiar story themes and link to own experiences in same or similar form.
- T. 10 To use story structure to write about own experiences in same or similar form.
- T. 11 To use language of time (see 'Grammar and punctuation') to structure a sequence of events, such as 'when I had finished …', 'suddenly …', 'after that …'.

Grammar and punctuation (sentence-level work)

- S. 2 To find examples, in fiction and non-fiction, of words and phrases that link sentences, such as 'after', 'meanwhile', 'during', 'before', 'then', 'next', 'after a while'.
- S. 4 To re-read own writing for sense and punctuation.

Spelling and vocabulary (word-level work)

- W. 10 New words from reading linked to particular topics, to build individual collections of personal interest or significant words.

Lesson 1

Resources
- book: *Hurrah for Ethelyn* by Babette Cole
- Sentence sequencing worksheet (Worksheet 13, page 113)
- glue and scissors

Introduction and whole-class activity

Read the story *Hurrah for Ethelyn*. Let the pupils follow the text as you read it. Ask the pupils to pick out the main events in the story.
- Who are the main characters?
- How was Ethelyn treated in the story? Was this fair?
- Can the pupils recall any occasions when they may have been treated in a similar way?
- Is this kind of behaviour hurtful? How does it make the pupils feel?
- Why do they think someone might be hurtful like that?

Discuss hurtful things that pupils say and do to each other, things that the pupils have said themselves and things that have been said to them, by peers, parents or teachers, for instance.

Make sure the pupils know the meaning of all of the vocabulary. Pay particular attention to 'scholarship', 'nasty', 'bullies', 'jealous', 'dormousery', 'surgeon', 'Toerat'. Why were these words chosen?

Group activity

Give out a copy of the sentence sequencing worksheet (Worksheet 13) to each pupil.

Ask the pupils, in groups, to sequence the sentences into the correct order. The pupils then cut and stick them in their books. (Alternatively, pupils can show the sequence of the story by drawing a series of pictures.)

Plenary

The pupils pick out aspects of the story where Ethelyn was treated fairly or unfairly.

This lesson could continue as part of a circle time activity where the pupils discuss incidents in their lives where they have been treated fairly or unfairly.

Lesson 2

Resource
- book: *Hurrah for Ethelyn* by Babette Cole
- prepare a set of ten cards containing negative, hurtful statements, such as:

Shut up!	You're not my friend!
You're thick!	Stop copying me!
Go away!	Get out of my way!
You are stupid!	What are you looking at?
No, you can't play!	You're really horrible!

Introduction and whole-class activity

Read pages 7–18 of *Hurrah for Ethelyn*. Ask the pupils to look for words and phrases that show the passing of time. They should be able to find 'after', 'until', 'eventually' and 'during'.

- Where do these words usually occur?
- How do they change the story?

Group activity

Give out the cards containing hurtful statements to the pupils in groups. Ask a pupil from each group to read out the hurtful statement. As each card is read out, each group needs to think of a positive way of saying what is written on the card. The pupils discuss and decide on the best alternative and write it down. The pupils should be encouraged to begin their new, positive statement with 'I feel' or 'I think' or 'I am'. This helps them to focus on themselves and how they feel, rather than being negative about the other person.

Each group can read out their new, positive statement. For example 'Shut up!' could be replaced with 'Please don't talk, I'm trying to work.' 'You are stupid!' could become 'I have another idea!', and so on. The pupils will have many and varied ideas.

Next, ask the pupils to think about other 'put-downs' and things said to them that they find insulting. This can be done individually or in groups or pairs. Anonymously, the pupils put their insults into a box. Each one is picked out and read by the teacher and alternative comments are suggested.

Insults to do with race, culture, size etc. need particular care, because they are sensitive issues. The aim is to encourage the pupils to respond rather than not say anything. But the response should be specific.

Rather than saying 'You sad cow', encourage the pupils to say 'I'm angry because you kicked me!'.

Each put-down reversal should begin with 'I feel', 'I am' or 'I think'.

Plenary

Do the pupils feel happier with the positive statements? Do they think they could use them in situations where they may feel angry or frustrated? How could this make class time and playtime more pleasant? Is it better to insult someone or to say what you really think or feel in a positive way?

Lesson 3

Resources
- book: *Hurrah for Ethelyn* by Babette Cole

Introduction and whole-class activity

Read pages 1–9 of *Hurrah for Ethelyn*. Ask individual pupils to point out where capital letters are used in the text. (It may be necessary to enlarge sections of the text for this activity.) Ask the pupils why they think Ethelyn initially didn't fit in at her new school.
- What was special about the school?
- Could anybody go there?
- What does it mean to get a scholarship?

The purpose of this lesson is to show pupils that although we are different in many ways, we are all equal. People belong to different groups, such as for music, dance, sport etc. Sometimes people have a dislike for particular groups of people without valid reason. Sometimes people get jealous if they see other people belonging to a group, so they may bully them to make themselves feel better.

You will need space for this activity.

Ask the pupils to find and stand in groups according to the following characteristics. Pupils with:
- the same age
- the same birthday month
- the same hair length (perhaps have three groups: long, short and medium)
- the same teacher
- the same way of getting to school
- the same favourite animal, colour, television programme etc.

Give the pupils a moment or two within their group each time.

Now consider the following questions in discussion with the pupils.
1. Were the same pupils always in the same groups?
2. Were all the groups always equal in number?
3. Were there any groups with only one child in them? Did this make a difference? How? Why? How did it feel?
4. When was it possible to guess which group pupils belonged to and when was it not possible?
5. Did pupils feel better when they were in a big group together? Why?
6. Did any of the pupils feel unhappy at any time? Why?
7. How could things have been made better?

Group activity

Next, ask the pupils to draw a picture of the group in which they felt happiest and unhappiest. Ask the pupils to write the reasons why underneath.

Plenary

Share the pupils' work. Can the pupils suggest ways of helping each other when they feel unhappy in the future?

Lesson 4

Resources
- book: *Frog and the Stranger* by Max Velthuijs
- Incident worksheet (Worksheet 14, page 114)

Introduction and whole-class activity

Read the story *Frog and the Stranger*. Discuss what the characters in the story thought of Rat. Ask the pupils why they think the characters had these thoughts.
- What do we think about rats? How do we know? Are they all the same?
- What do we think about dogs, horses etc.? Are they all the same?
- Are people/pupils all the same?
- How does the rat deal with the dislike shown him?
- How do we deal with inappropriate behaviour?
- Do we say things that are not true about our friends when we are angry with them?

Read the first 13 pages of the story again slowly, and let the pupils pick out the words used by Pig, Duck and Frog before they have even met and talked to him.

Draw a table with the three headings Pig, Duck and Frog on the board, and as you read each page, ask the pupils to tell you the words used by the three animals that suggest their feelings and thoughts about Rat.

You should expect to end up with this.

Pig	Duck	Frog
stranger	thieving	wonderful smell
filthy	cheeky	cosy
dirty	lazy	nice fellow
be careful	rude	impressed
no business here		
stole wood		
disapproved		
different		

Why is it wrong for the animals to make these assumptions before meeting Rat? Do we ever do this?

Group activity

Ask the pupils how they feel when people make assumptions about them.

Give out the Incident worksheet (Worksheet 14). Carefully read the first question and each possible response to the pupils. Ask the pupils to place the responses in order, beginning with the most appropriate, numbering each response from 1 to 5.

Plenary

Share the pupils' results on the board. Have all the pupils come up with same order?

Do the pupils think they would really respond as they have said, if such an incident happened, or is it more difficult to respond in the right way when you are feeling angry? What could help us to respond in the right way?

Lesson 5

Resources
- book: *Frog and the Stranger* by Max Velthuijs
- Resolutions worksheet (Worksheet 15, page 115)

Introduction and whole-class activity

Read pages 14–20 of *Frog and the Stranger*.
- Why did Pig, Duck and Hare change their mind about the way they felt about Rat?
- Do they think Rat was trying to please the other animals, or was he just simply being himself?
- Which animals do they think changed the most during this story? In what way did they change?
- Do they think the animals would have behaved differently if another new animal arrived?

Give the pupils the Resolutions worksheet. Read the first situation on the Resolutions worksheet. Use shared writing to model the way in which the resolution could be found for the first situation.

Group activity

In their groups, ask the pupils to come up with resolutions for the other situations.

Plenary

Ask each group to share their resolutions and say whether these would be easy or difficult to follow in a real-life situation.

Lesson 6

Resources
- role-play cards (Worksheet 16, page 116)

Introduction and whole-class activity

The pupils will be taking part in role-play activities. It may be necessary to remind the pupils about the importance of listening and being sensitive to one another within their groups.

Group activity

Read the role-play cards to the class (Worksheet 16). Give a card to each group. Within that group, ask one or more of the pupils to imagine they are the one who is being bullied. They then talk to the group about how they feel. Ask the rest of the group to suggest ways of solving the problem.

Plenary

Ask the pupils to share their fears and the solutions from their group. By this stage, many issues will have been brought up. Ask the pupils to suggest ideas for stories of their own, dealing with one of the many issues based on bullying. Tell the pupils that you want them to write a story about being bullied or being a bully. They will need to think carefully about how they would feel and try to describe this. They can consider the characters in the two stories used this week. Suggestions for suitable vocabulary that they may want to use can be recorded on the board.

Lesson 7

Resources	■ books:
	  – *Hurrah for Ethelyn* by Babette Cole
	  – *Frog and the Stranger* by Max Velthuijs

Introduction and whole-class activity	Choose one of the texts and ask the pupils to point out capital letters and full stops and explain why they are used. ■ What other punctuation is used in the text? Revise the use of time words, showing the passing of time. ■ Can the pupils think of any more? Write their suggestions on the board. Read through the list of words about bullying from the previous lesson. ■ Are the pupils clear about the meaning of the words? ■ Is there any new vocabulary to add?
Group activity	Ask the pupils to plan and write their own stories about bullying or being bullied. (This may need additional time for completion.) Many of the pupils will immediately have ideas for their stories. Others will need to be guided more carefully with a writing frame or modelled writing led by the teacher. For some pupils the basis for a story will need to be planned with the teacher.
Plenary	Ask some of the pupils to share their story introductions. **Note:** *Some of the activities used in Lessons 2, 3, 4, 5 and 6 are based on ideas from* Our World, Our Rights *by Amnesty International.*

Worksheet 13

Sentence sequencing

Ethelyn became a brilliant brain surgeon.

Tina got stuck.

She won a scholarship.

Ethelyn wrote to her brother.

Tina Toerat was a bully.

Tina Toerat and her friends called her rude names.

Ethelyn was a clever rat.

They put Miss Nibble's cheese under Ethelyn's bed.

Ethelyn operated on Toerat's brain.

Worksheet 14

Incident worksheet

Your friend is reading your favourite book. You want it too. **What do you do?**	**You have been called horrible names by someone in your class.** **What do you do?**
☐ Grab the book ☐ Ask them for it ☐ Be rude to your friend ☐ Scream until the teacher gives it to you ☐ Take turns	☐ Call them names too ☐ Tell the teacher ☐ Look away ☐ Punch them ☐ Cry

Worksheet 15

Resolutions worksheet

You have just got a computer game. Your best friend wants to play it but only one can play at a time.

What do you do?

Some pupils in your class are playing football in the playground. You want to join in.

What do you do?

You see some money on the classroom floor. You pick it up and put it in your pocket. Later another child in your class is in tears because she has lost her bus fare home. The teacher asks if anyone in the class can help.

What do you do?

You are playing with your friends in the park. They are saying nasty things about another friend in your class.

What do you say?

Worksheet 16

Role-play cards

You see people whispering.

Someone takes your dinner money.

Someone calls you names.

You have no one to play with.

You join a group of friends and they stop talking.

The 'bullies' are waiting to get you on the way home.

Someone pushes you in the line.

Someone pulls faces at you.

Children's rights

This series of lessons is suitable for use in Year 4 and Year 5. If you are following the Literacy Strategy, it is particularly designed to fit with Year 4, term 3.

Learning objectives

The following objectives are covered in this series of lessons.

Comprehension and composition (text-level work)

T. 16 To read, compare and evaluate examples of arguments and discussions, such as a letter to the press, articles, discussion of issues in books, for example concerning the environment or animal welfare.

T. 17 How arguments are presented, for example: ordering points to link them together so that one follows on from another; how statistics, graphs etc. can be used to support arguments.

T. 18 From examples of persuasive writing, to investigate how style and vocabulary are used to convince the intended reader.

T. 20 To summarise a sentence or paragraph by identifying the most important elements and re-wording them in a limited number of words.

T. 21 To assemble and sequence points in order to plan the presentation of a point of view, for example on hunting or school rules.

T. 22 To use writing frames if necessary to back up points of view, for example on hunting or school rules.

T. 23 To present a point of view in writing, for instance in the form of a letter, a report or a script, linking points persuasively and selecting style and vocabulary appropriate to the reader.

T. 24 To summarise in writing the key ideas from, for example, a paragraph or chapter.

Lesson 1

Introduction and whole-class activity

Ask the pupils about the things that they need every day, giving prompts such as food, drink, clothing, space to work or play, communication, health, transport etc. Write up their suggestions on the board.

Group activity

Ask the pupils in pairs to write down the suggestions under two headings, Needs and Wants. (It may be necessary to include an additional space for anything that the pupils feel doesn't fit under Needs and Wants.) The pairs then make a group of four to compare and discuss results.

Is one list longer than the other? Why is that? Make a list of the pupils' results on the board.

Are there any areas where the pupils disagree?

Plenary

Ask the pupils to look at the list of needs. Encourage them to focus on things they really need to live. What do they think everyone has a right to? What is everyone entitled to?

You may have to prompt the pupils to consider family, shelter, safety, education, play, medicine, friendships etc. Mark the ones the whole class considers are essential for survival. Should these be rights for all children or just children in the class? Are there any other things that all children should be entitled to? Collect all the pupils' suggestions and write them on a chart, to be placed in a prominent place in the classroom for use or reference in future lessons.

Lesson 2

Resources

- list of Children's Rights Articles (Worksheet 17, page 124)

Introduction and whole-class activity

Tell the pupils about the international law called The Convention on the Rights of the Child.

It was written in 1989 and came into force in 1990. All the countries in the world have agreed to it except the USA and Somalia. All the countries of the world try to make the law work.

These rights for children are about what children are allowed to do, and what the people responsible for children have to do to make sure they are happy, healthy and safe. Look at the list of Articles from the Convention (Worksheet 17).

Choose a selection from the list (or all of them if time allows) and ask the pupils to explain what they think each one means and why it is important.

Group activities

Give each group a copy of the Articles. (You may give all to some groups and a selection to others). Ask each group to select three Articles that they think are particularly important and note down their reasons.

Plenary

Each group shares their top three Articles, and their reasons for choosing them, with the class. Which were the most popular Articles chosen? Why was this? Do the pupils think that all children are given these rights?

Lesson 3

Resources
- book: *For Every Child* by Caroline Castle
- enlarged copy of the text from *For Every Child* (Worksheet 18, page 125)
- sugar paper

Introduction and whole-class activity

Read the book *For Every Child*, showing and sharing the pictures.

Re-read the book, following the enlarged copy of the text. Ask individual pupils to give the key point brought up on each page. Are there any points the pupils don't understand? Write the key points on sugar paper in note form. Now ask individual pupils to explain what each key point means in their own words. Look at the way in which each 'right' has been introduced, for example: 'Allow us …', 'All children shall …', 'Teach us …', 'No one …'. How is this more effective than beginning each page in the same way, for example with 'All children …'? Now take one of the points written on the sugar paper and model a paragraph expanding on the point to show how it relates to everyday life.

Group activity

Choosing three or four points from the sugar paper, ask the pupils to write their own expanded paragraphs. (A discussion about the impact of the pictures in the book could be used as the basis for an art activity.)

Plenary

Cut the sugar paper into 14 pieces with one key point on each piece. Give these out randomly to 14 pupils. Ask individual pupils to read one of the paragraphs they have written to the class. As they read out their paragraph, the pupil with the matching key point on the sugar paper holds it up in the air. Which of the rights did the pupils feel were the most important? Which ones affected the way they felt?

Lesson 4

Resources
- Charles's story (*It's Our Right*) (Worksheet 19, page 127)
- Charles's story worksheets (Worksheets 20 and 21, pages 129 and 130)
- 14 pieces of sugar paper from previous lesson
- glue and scissors

Introduction and whole-class activity

Read the text *Charles's story*.
- What are the important things Charles has to think about in his everyday life?
- How do these compare with what we have to consider?
- How does Charles deal with the things that we take for granted in our lives, such as food, shelter and education?

Give out the 14 pieces of sugar paper to pupils in the class. Which of these rights does Charles have? (Get the pupils to hold high the rights he has and lower those he doesn't have.) Should he be entitled to these rights?

Group activity	Give out the two worksheets on pages 129 and 130 (Worksheets 20 and 21). Ask the pupils to cut and stick the rights from the first worksheet into the appropriate section on the second worksheet under the following headings: ■ Yes, Charles has these rights ■ No, Charles does not have these rights ■ I'm not sure
Plenary	Share the pupils' results. Go through the worksheets and discuss the following questions: 1 What rights does Charles have? 2 What rights should Charles have? 3 What are the things Charles likes about his life? 4 What does he want to do in the future? 5 What things make life difficult for Charles? 6 Which Children's Rights does Uganda appear to support? 7 Which Children's Rights do the pupils think the UK supports?

Lesson 5

Introduction and whole-class activity	Ask the pupils why they think some countries have not signed up for the Convention. Do they think it is hard for countries to stick to it?
	
	Ask the pupils to design a poster showing the A–Z of Children's Rights (or an A–Z frieze.) Each letter should represent one or part of one of the articles from the UN Convention on the Rights of the Child, or any aspect from the book *For Every Child*, for example:
	
	    Adults should do what is best for us
	    Be kind to us and help us in times of trouble
	    Care for us when we are sick
	
	and so on.
	
	The pupils can work in pairs or groups to plan the wording for the posters. Extra time will be needed to complete the posters and to include pictures to represent some of the points. These posters could be used as part of an assembly.

Plenary	Each pupil can read his or her most effective statement. Alternatively, each pupil can read one statement, starting with A and ending with Z.

Lesson 6

This lesson clearly covers a sensitive issue. Here are some points to consider before doing the lesson.

- Think about the content of the lesson, the possible outcomes and reactions of individual children, and how you will deal with them.
- Ensure that systems are in place for children who may need support.

This lesson may be omitted if you are unsure how to deal with the outcomes.

Resources
- book: *For Every Child* by Caroline Castle (opened at Right number 19)

Introduction and whole-class activity

Ask the pupils if they know what NSPCC stands for. The NSPCC run many campaigns to help protect children. Ask the pupils if they know about any of the campaigns. The NSPCC supports children who suffer from abuse or those who need help or protection. The NSPCC is hugely disappointed because in the UK the government still allows children to be hit by their parents. The NSPCC, other organisations and individuals are urging the government to give the same protection from assault to children as adults receive by law, so that no child should ever be hit. Show the pupils the picture from *For Every Child* showing Right number 19. Ask the pupils to give reasons why they think hitting a child should be allowed and why hitting a child should not be allowed. Make a list of the points on the board.

Group activity

The pupils present a debate on 'Adults should not be allowed to smack children'. Divide the class into two teams: one team will be for the issue and one team against. Then separate each team into smaller groups. You may have reasons for putting pupils into particular groups or teams. Each small group will come up with a statement supporting their team's side of the argument. Remind the pupils that they do not have to agree with their team. What is important is to present a convincing argument. Encourage the pupils to use the points collected by the class during the whole-class activity. Each group then votes for a spokesperson to present their points for their team.

Plenary

The pupils from each team present their points to the class. Those not directly involved in the presentation can vote for the team they feel is the more convincing. It is important that the pupils have the opportunity to share their thoughts and feelings, in particular if they had to support an argument with which they did not agree. How easy was it to convince people to think in a particular way, even if they didn't believe it themselves?

Lesson 7

Resources
- quotation from Liam O'Neill, 13, Ireland (*Stand Up For Your Rights*, 1998) (Worksheet 22, page 131)
- list of addresses and websites

Introduction and whole-class activity

Read the quotation by Liam O'Neill to the class. Ask the pupils whether or not they agree with Liam. Have they ever been in a situation where they have felt afraid to speak the truth? Ask them who they think has the power to make things better or worse for children in other parts of the world. How could pupils influence those who have the power to make changes?

Discuss letter writing as a useful tool in persuading organisations or individuals with power to change the way they do things. Organisations such as Amnesty International encourage people to write to others who are imprisoned in order to give them support. Organisations such as UNICEF support children's education all over the world. You may want the children to follow the same format, writing to a specified person or group on one particular point, or you may wish to give a variety of options from which the pupils can choose. It may be possible for some of the class to write letters to find out more information about Children's Rights, while others write directly to world leaders persuading them to change the way children are treated. A writing frame may help the pupils to write persuasively and to back up their points of view with examples. Formal letter writing may need to be revised, and the teacher could also model the writing of a formal letter.

Plenary

The pupils should have decided who they are going to write to and be very clear on the expected outcomes of their letter writing. This could be shared with the class.

This activity will take more than one session. Responses to the pupils' letters can lead to a greater involvement with particular charities or organisations. The pupils may be encouraged to continue to explore these areas and share them over the following few weeks.

There are also a number of very good websites which some of the pupils could visit.

Addresses and websites

Addresses

- Children's Legal Centre, University of Essex, Wivenhoe Park, Colchester CO4 3SQ
- Child Poverty Action Group, 4th Floor, 1–5 Bath Street, London EC1V 9PY
- Children's Rights Office, 235 Shaftesbury Avenue, London WC2H 8EL
- Oxfam Campaigns, 274 Banbury Road, Oxford OX2 7DZ
- Save the Children, Mary Datchelor House, 17 Grove Lane, London SE5 8RD
- UNICEF, 55 Lincoln's Inn Fields, London WC2A 3NB
- Amnesty International, 99–119 Rosebery Avenue, London, EC1R 4RE
- NSPCC, 42 Curtain Road, London, EC2A 3NH

Websites

www.nspcc.org	For the pupils there is a good section called Kids' Zone.
www.unicef.org	This site contains the complete version of the Convention.
www.essex.ac.uk/clc	The site of the Children's Legal Centre, with some interesting information.
www.antislavery.org	Contains news on children's rights around the world

Worksheet 17

Selected Articles from the UN Convention on the Rights of the Child

Article 3
Adults should do what is best for you.

Article 6
You have the right to live.

Article 14
You have the right to think what you like and be whatever religion you want to be. Your parents should help you learn what is right and wrong.

Article 15
You have the right to make friends.

Article 17
You have the right to collect information from radios, newspapers, television, books etc., from all around the world.

Article 19
No one should hurt you in any way.

Article 24
You have a right to good health.

Article 27
You have the right to food, clothes, and a place to live.

Article 28
You have a right to education.

Article 30
You have the right to enjoy your own culture, practise your own religion and use your own language.

Article 31
You have the right to play.

Article 37
You should not be put in prison.

Article 35
No one is allowed to kidnap or sell you.

Worksheet 18

Text from *For Every Child*, by Caroline Castle

Whoever we are, wherever we live, these rights belong to all children under the sun and the moon and the stars, whether we live in cities or towns or villages, or in mountains or valleys or deserts or forests or jungles. Anywhere and everywhere in the big, wide world, these are the rights of every child.

Understand that all children are precious. Pick us up if we fall down and if we are lost lend us your hand. Give us the things we need to make us happy and strong, and always do your best for us whenever we are in your care.

All children should be allowed to live and to grow … and grow … and grow … until we are grown up and can decide things for ourselves.

Max, Zahra, Betty, Juan, Suyin, Reza, Paolo, Yair, Yoko, Mohammed … Every one of us shall have a name and a land to call our own.

Keep our families together, and if we have no family, look after us and love us just the same.

Allow us to tell you what we are thinking or feeling. Whether our voices are big or small, whether we whisper or shout it, or paint, draw, mime or sign it – listen to us and hear what we say.

Worksheet 18 *continued*

No one on Earth has the right to hurt us, not even our mums and dads. Protect us always from anyone who would be cruel.

If we are disabled, either in body or in mind, treasure us especially and give us the care we need to live happily in the world.

Watch over us. Wrap us up against the cold and rain, and give us shade from the hot sun. Make sure we have enough to eat and drink and if we are sick, nurse and comfort us.

Teach us all to read and write and teach us well so we grow up to be the best we can at whatever we wish to do. Take care of our Earth – the flowers, the trees, the rivers, the seas – and teach us how to care for it in our turn.

All children will have time to play and time to rest when we are tired.

In times of war do not make us part of any battle, but shelter us and protect us from all harm.

Allow us to say our own prayers in our own words, whether in churches or temples, synagogues or mosques, chapels or shrines or any other place a prayer may be said to our own God. And let us sing and dance and dress in the ways of our own people.

Do your best to let everyone know that, whoever we are, wherever we live, these are the rights of every child.

Worksheet 19

Charles's story from *It's Our Right*

Hi! My name is Charles Senyange and I am 12, nearly 13. I live with about twenty other boys in an old wagon in the railway yard in Kampala, a city in Uganda. I have to live there because my parents were killed by soldiers three years ago and I ran away and hid here.

We sleep on the floor of the wagon on newspapers, but I also have some empty cardboard boxes and a bed sheet which I have to keep hidden in a safe place during the day or they would be stolen.

I do have a very good friend and we help to look after each other. His name is Musa Umani and we keep each other warm at night when it gets very cold in the wagon.

In the morning I usually go straight to the city market about 10 minutes walk away. It is here that all the lorries arrive with loads of goods to sell. I often pick up loose bananas from the floor where they have fallen and sell them. Sometimes I sell soap which I buy cheaply from one of the lorry drivers.

For my breakfast, which I buy from the hot food stalls in the market, I have black coffee with sugar, and some cassava with beans. For lunch I may have matoke and rice. When I have earned a lot I may buy some meat.

© Chris Kington Publishing and Oxfam GB 2002

Worksheet 19 *continued*

I have one pair of shorts and one shirt which I wash once a week in the river with a bit of soap. I also have a pair of shoes – I found them on the rubbish pile.

The police don't like boys like me working in the market. They think we're going to make trouble. Sometimes they come and chase us away so we have to be on the lookout for them. If they catch us they sometimes take us to the police station and beat us, or they may send us to Naguru, a boys' home. I don't like Naguru because we are treated just like prisoners; we can't walk or go out, and besides, I don't like the food there.

I like my life in the wagon and working in the market – it's a lot better than going to school. I went to school when I was younger and that's where I learnt to speak English.

When I get older I hope to have my own stall at the market and make enough money to rent a house.

Worksheet 20

Charles's rights

| All children have rights | All children have the right to be taken care of by parents or family members |

| All children have the right to be protected | All children have the right to be given help and protection if they have no family or parents |

| All children have the right to a name | All children have the right to be helped if someone is being cruel or violent towards them |

| All children have the right to a home | All children have the right to education and to play |

| All children have the right to medicine if they are sick | All children have the right to follow their own religion and not suffer from racial abuse |

| All children have the right to be looked after |

Worksheet 21

Charles's rights

Yes, Charles has these rights	No, Charles does not have these rights	I'm not sure

Worksheet 22

Quotation from Liam O'Neill

Last week I read in the newspaper about someone who had been put in prison for saying something against his government. This is so wrong. Everyone should be able to think and say what they like, as long as they aren't lying. If you believe something from the bottom of your heart – say it and don't be afraid.

Liam O'Neill, 13, Ireland

Nelson Mandela: biography and autobiography

This series of lessons is suitable for use in Year 6. If you are following the Literacy Strategy, it is particularly designed to fit in with Year 6 Term 1.

Learning objectives

The following objectives covered in this series of lessons.

Comprehension and composition (text-level work)

T. 3   To articulate personal responses to literature, identifying why and how a text affects the reader

T. 5   To contribute constructively to shared discussion about literature, responding to and building on the views of others

T. 11 To distinguish between biography and autobiography:
- recognising the effect on the reader of the choice between first and third person
- distinguishing between fact, opinion and fiction
- distinguishing between implicit and explicit points of view and how these can differ

T. 14 To develop the skills of biographical and autobiographical writing in role, adopting distinctive voices such as those of historical characters, through, for instance:
- preparing a CV
- composing a biographical account based on research
- describing a person from different perspectives – for example, police description, school report, newspaper obituary.

Lesson 1

Resources
- a selection of biographical and autobiographical books written by and about significant people
- if available, copies of the following books:
  - Nelson Mandela's autobiography *Long Walk to Freedom*
  - *Nelson Mandela* by Benjamin Pogrund
  - *A Desire to Serve the People* by Mary Benson
  - *Nelson Mandela: A Biography* by Martin Meredith
- enlarged texts of extracts from biographies of Nelson Mandela (Worksheets 23, 25 and 26, pages 138, 141 and 144)
- photocopies of biographical texts on Nelson Mandela cut randomly into paragraphs (Worksheets 23, 25 and 26)
- photocopies of the Information worksheet (Worksheet 24, page 140)
- one enlarged copy of the Information worksheet (Worksheet 24)
- glossary, page 154.

Introduction and whole-class activity

Show the selection of biographies and autobiographies to the class. Ask the pupils questions such as:
- What kind of books are these?
- Which books are written in the first person, which are written in the third person?
- What do they tell us?
- Why would a person choose to write about another person?
- Would it be an easy task? Why?
- Pick out the books written about Nelson Mandela. Who is Nelson Mandela? Why would a person choose to write about him?

Read the first text by Mary Benson, *A Desire to Serve the People* (Worksheet 23), telling of Nelson's life as a young boy. Show the pupils an enlarged copy of the Information worksheet (Worksheet 24).

Go through the text again slowly with the pupils and ask them to decide which information should go into which box on the worksheet. Make notes in the appropriate box as suggested by the pupils. Model the way in which notes can be made from the text without writing whole sentences.

Group activity

Give out the Information worksheets (Worksheet 24) to the pupils. Give out the photocopied texts on Nelson Mandela (Worksheets 23, 25 and 26), cut randomly into paragraphs. Ask the pupils, in pairs, to find out as much information as they can to write up on their worksheets. Some of the information may have already been shared. Can the pupils find out anything new? Encourage the pupils to use the glossary where necessary.

Plenary

Bring the class back together again with their worksheets. Can the pupils add any additional information to what has already been recorded? Was there any contradictory information? Have the pupils remembered the difference between biography and autobiography? Which is written in the first and which in the third person?

Lesson 2

Resources
- class dictionary
- Extract 1 from *Long Walk to Freedom* by Nelson Mandela (Worksheet 27, page 146)
- Fact, fiction and opinion worksheets (Worksheets 28 and 29, pages 148 and 149)

Introduction and whole-class activity

Show the selection of books again. Ask the pupils:

1. What is the difference between the books written about Nelson Mandela and the book written by Nelson Mandela?
2. Why would someone want to write about their own life for others to read?
3. What can you learn about a person by reading about his or her life?

Write the words 'biography' and 'autobiography' on the board. Ask a couple of pupils to look up and read out the dictionary definition of each word. Make a list for each with ideas from the pupils. For biography, you should expect suggestions such as these:

- tells us about the person's environment
- what effect that person has had on others
- shows that the author knows a lot about the person
- telling facts about a real person's life
- showing the truth, the person's strengths and weaknesses
- tells us why this person is interesting
- tells us how the writer feels about the person
- is written in the third person.

For autobiography, as well as some of the above, you should also expect:

- the main person in the book is also the writer of the book
- shows the emotions and feelings of the writer
- tells of the people who have had the biggest influence on the author's life
- recounts the main significant events that have changed and influenced the author
- is written in the first person.

Read the extract from Nelson Mandela's autobiography, *Long Walk to Freedom* (Worksheet 27). Use the glossary (Worksheet 30) where appropriate.

Group activity

Show the pupils the Fact, fiction and opinion Worksheet 28.

Read out two statements about Nelson Mandela. The pupils need to decide which is fact and which is fiction.

- 'Nelson Mandela was born in South Africa.'
- 'Nelson Mandela was born in South America.'

Write each statement in the correct column.

Say, 'I think Nelson Mandela is a very courageous man'. Ask the pupils where they think that should go.

Give the pupils a sheet of statements, some fact and some fiction (Worksheet 29). The pupils should cut them up and stick them in the correct column of Worksheet 28.

Once the pupils have completed the worksheet, they will need to think about their own opinion of Nelson Mandela. They may already have their own ideas for this section; if not, they will need to consider what they have learnt and what they now think about him from the information they have read.

Plenary

Check through the statements. Did all the pupils put the statements in the correct column? Do they all understand the difference between fact, fiction and opinion?

Ask some of the pupils to share their opinions of Nelson Mandela. What made the pupils have these opinions? What influenced them?

Lesson 3

Resources
- extract from *Nelson Mandela* by Benjamin Pogrund (Worksheet 26, page 144)

Introduction and whole-class activity

Ask the pupils questions about biographies and autobiographies, for example:
- Who can write them?
- Why would a person choose to write a biography or autobiography?
- What makes the lives of certain people so interesting?
- What can you learn about a person by reading about their life?
- What can you learn about yourself?
- What makes a best seller?

Read the extract from Benjamin Pogrund's biography of Nelson Mandela. Add any additional notes to the original Information worksheet from Lesson 1 (Worksheet 24). Referring to the biographies and autobiographies, how would the pupils choose which one to read? How does the writer make the reader stay interested, without exaggerating?

Model the opening of a biography of Nelson Mandela with the class. Consider the choice of vocabulary, the style, and ways in which to engage the reader.

Group activity

Ask the pupils to begin their own biographies of Nelson Mandela, using the information from the previous lessons. Additional time will be needed to complete these biographies.

Plenary

The pupils share their favourite sentences or phrases that they have used to grip the reader.

Lesson 4

Before the lesson, the children could undertake some research into their early lives. This would enable them to appreciate how people writing their autobiography rely on families supplying information about their early years. The pupils could draw themselves a grid with three boxes across the page for each year of their lives. Using headings for each column, they could find out for each year information relevant to:

- themselves (when they walked, talked, went to school, and so on)
- their families (when sisters or brothers were born, when an aunt came from India to stay, when a grandparent died, and so on)
- the world (for example, when Nelson Mandela became president of South Africa, when he retired, when wars happened) – whatever national or international events seem relevant to them and their families.

Resources
- Extract 2 from *Long Walk to Freedom* by Nelson Mandela (Worksheet 31)
- Facts about me worksheet (Worksheet 30)

Introduction and whole-class activity

Recap on the purpose of biographies and autobiographies.
- Whose biography or autobiography would the pupils like to read?
- Would any of the pupils like to write a biography?
- Who would they choose to write about?
- Does the person have to be famous?

Read the extracts from Nelson Mandela's autobiography. Have the pupils noticed any discrepancies or contradictions between the biographies and autobiography?

Show an enlarged copy of the Facts about me worksheet (Worksheet 30) to the class. Model information to include on the worksheet, including as many interesting points as possible, without exaggerating.

Group activity

Give the pupils a 'Facts about me' worksheet (Worksheet 30) to complete. Again, the worksheet is for making notes rather than writing in full sentences. The pupils may need additional time to complete the worksheet.

Plenary

Ask the pupils to share any interesting facts about themselves, from the 'Facts about me' worksheet and any additional research done at home.

Lesson 5

Resources
- Extract 1 from *Long Walk to Freedom* by Nelson Mandela (Worksheet 27)

Introduction and whole-class activity

Ask the pupils whether or not they think people write autobiographies on their own. Take one or two of the pupils' 'Facts about me' worksheets and/or additional research done at home, and model one or two paragraphs of an autobiography. Encourage the pupils to suggest vocabulary and phrases to maintain the interest of the reader. Pick out one or two sentences from Nelson Mandela's autobiography that may inspire the pupil's own writing.

1. What information can the pupils recall?
2. Why have they remembered those points?

Brainstorm opening lines for the pupil's autobiographies.

Group activity

Using all the information the pupils have collected so far, ask the pupils to begin writing their own autobiographies.

Plenary

Ask the pupils to share opening lines. Which ones are the most powerful? Which openings would you like to read to the end? Why?

Worksheet 23

From *A Desire to Serve the People*, by Mary Benson

When a son was born to Chief Henry Gadla Mandela and his wife, Nonqaphi, on 18th July 1918, they gave him the Xhosa name of Rolihlahla and, because it was the fashion to have a European name, preferably a heroic one, they also called him Nelson.

The boy and his three sisters lived in the family kraal of whitewashed huts not far from Umtata in the Transkei. Although the Mandelas were members of the royal family of the Thembu people, Nelson, like most African children, herded sheep and cattle and helped with the ploughing.

As a young boy he was tall for his age, and was a fast runner. He hunted buck and, when hungry, stole mealie cobs from the maize fields. He loved the countryside with its grassy rolling hills and the stream which flowed eastward to the Indian Ocean.

At night, under Africa's brilliant stars, everyone used to gather around a big open fire to listen to the elders of the tribe. The boy was fascinated by the tales told by these bearded old men. Tales about the 'good old days before the coming of the white man', and tales about the brave acts performed by their ancestors, in defending their country against the European invaders.

Worksheet 23 *continued*

Those tales, said Mandela many years later when he was on trial for his life, stirred in him a desire to serve his people in their struggle to be free. A desire which eventually led to his becoming the most famous political prisoner of our time – a prisoner with songs written about him and streets named after him. How appropriate that Nelson Mandela's Xhosa name, Rolihlahla, means 'stirring up trouble'.

When Nelson first went to school – a school for African children – it was a shock to find the history books described only white heroes, and referred to his people as savages and cattle thieves. All the same he was eager for western education, and proud that his great-grandfather had given land on which to build a mission school. Even when fellow-pupils teased him about his clothes, cast-offs from his father, he pretended not to mind.

Worksheet 24

Information worksheet

Nelson's family	Description of Nelson
Food	Description of the environment
Entertainment	School life

Worksheet 25

From *Nelson Mandela: A Biography* by Martin Meredith

Mandela was born in the simple surroundings of a peasant village on the banks of the Mbashe River in Thembuland. But for his royal connections, his childhood would have been no different from those of many others there. His great-grandfather Ngubengcuka, however, was a Thembu king. And although Mandela was descended from only a minor branch of the dynasty, his link with the Thembu royal family was to have a marked influence on both his character and his fortunes.

His father Gadla Henry Mphakanyiswa, was the village head at Mverzo, A tall, respected figure, he presided over local ceremonies and officiated at traditional rites for such occasions as births, marriages, funerals, harvests and initiation ceremonies. He had no formal education and could not read or write. But he had a keen sense of history and was valued as a counsellor to the royal family. He was also wealthy enough at one time to afford four wives and had thirteen children.

Mandela's mother, Nosekeni Nkedama, was the third of Gadla's wives. She bore four children, the eldest of whom, Mandela, was her only son but the youngest of Gadla's four sons. Like Gadla, she could neither read nor write. While Gadla adhered to the traditional Qaba faith, involving the worship of ancestral spirits, Nosekeni became a devout Christian, taking the name Fanny.

Worksheet 25 continued

The Xhosa name given to Mandela at his birth on the 18th July 1918 was Rolihalhla, which meant literally 'pulling the branch of a tree', but more colloquially 'troublemaker'. But the name by which he became popularly known was an English one, Nelson, given to him by an African teacher on the first day he attended school.

The landscape around Qunu – undulating hills, clear streams and lush pastures grazed by cattle, sheep and goats – made an indelible impression on Mandela. Qunu was the place where he felt his real roots lay. It was a settlement of beehive-shaped huts in a narrow valley where life continued much as it had done for generations past. There the peopled dyed their blankets with red ochre, a colour said to be beloved by ancestral spirits and the colour of their faith. There were few Christians in Qunu and those that were there stood out because of their Western-style clothes.

The Mandelas' homestead, like most others in Qunu, was simple. Their beehive huts – a cluster of three – were built without windows or chimneys. The floor was made of crusted earth taken from anthills and kept smooth with layers of fresh cow dung. There was no furniture, in the Western sense. Everyone slept on mats, without pillows, resting their heads on their arms. Smoke from the fire filtered through the grass roof. There was no opening other than a low doorway. Their diet was also simple, mainly maize, sorghum, beans and pumpkins grown in fields outside the village,

Worksheet 25 *continued*

and amasi, fermented milk stored in calabashes. Only a few wealthy families could afford luxuries like tea, coffee and sugar, bought from the local store.

Having four wives, each living in her own kraal several miles apart, Gadla visited them in turn, spending perhaps one week a month with each one.

Mandela's household in Qunu was often full of relatives. Uncles and aunts were as responsible for the children as the children's own parents and were referred to as 'little fathers' and 'little mothers'. Even though Mandela remembered his father for his stern countenance, Mandela tried to emulate him by rubbing white ash into his hair in imitation of the tuft of white hair above Gadla's forehead.

From the age of five, Mandela was set to work as a herdboy, looking after sheep and calves and learning the central role cattle play in Thembu society. Cattle were not only a source of meat and milk but the main medium of exchange and the measure of a tribesman's wealth. As the price of a bride was paid in cattle, without cattle there could be no marriage. Significant events like funerals were marked by their slaughter.

Much of Mandela's time was spent in the open veld in the company of members of his own age group, stick-throwing and fighting, gathering wild honey and fruits, trapping birds and small animals that could be roasted, and swimming in the cold streams.

Worksheet 26

From *Nelson Mandela,* by Benjamin Pogrund

Nelson Rolihlahla Mandela was born on July 18th 1918. In accordance with custom, he was given a 'European' name as well as his Xhosa name which means 'one who brings trouble on himself'.

His father Henry Mphakanyiswa Gadla, was a chief – wealthy enough to own a horse and have enough cattle for four wives. He had twelve children. Nelson was the son of his third wife, Nosekeni; she also had three daughters.

Mandela was born in the Transkei region of South Africa, in the small village of Qunu – a collection of beehive-shaped huts with thatch roofs, known as rondavels. His mother had three huts and Mandela lived with her and his three immediate sisters. One hut was used for sleeping, another for cooking and the third for storing grain and other food. Everyone slept on mats on the ground, without pillows. His mother, as a married woman, had her own field to tend and her own cattle kraal – an enclosure for cattle made from thorn bushes.

It was a quiet, tranquil existence. Qunu was a long way from anywhere, especially in those days when local roads, if they existed at all, were unsurfaced.

Worksheet 26 continued

Almost as soon as Nelson was old enough to walk properly, he had the job of helping to look after the family's precious cattle and goats. Relatives remember that he loved animals and, while herding, he would speak to each cow by its name, as if it was a friend.

His mother could not read or write, but Nelson had to be educated, and he started as a pupil at the local school. He was noted as quiet, industrious boy who did not live up to his Xhosa name. The school had classes for only the early years and in any event, when Nelson was ten, his father died and there was no money for any further education. So his father's nephew, Chief Jongintaba, took over.

In Xhosa society that was the natural thing to do. Jongintaba was the head of the Madiba clan. In terms of custom, all members of the clan were treated like people in the same family because they were all descended from the same ancestor. Mandela, or anyone else, could go to the home of any fellow Madiba member, whether in the same village or in a village miles away, and know that he would get food and shelter.

So in 1928, Nelson moved to the Great Place and shared a rondavel with his cousin, Justice. The school was a rough building, and two classes were held in one room at the same time. Nelson learnt English, Xhosa, Geography and History. He did not have writing books so wrote on slates.

Each day after school he and Justice went to the fields to look after the cattle, and to drive them back to the kraal in the evening for milking.

Worksheet 27

From Nelson Mandela's autobiography, *Long Walk to Freedom* (Extract 1)

My mother presided over three rondavels at Qunu which, as I remember, were always filled with the babies and children of my relations. In fact, I hardly recall any occasion as a child when I was alone. In African culture, the sons and daughters of one's aunts or uncles are considered brothers and sisters, not cousins. We do not make the same distinctions among relations practised by Europeans. We have no half-brothers or half-sisters. My mother's sister is my mother; my uncle's son is my brother.

Of my mother's three huts, one was used for cooking, one for sleeping and one for storage. In the hut in which we slept, there was no furniture.

We slept on mats and sat on the ground. I did not discover pillows until I went away to school. The stove on which my mother cooked was a three-legged iron pot that rested on a grate over a hole in the ground. Everything we ate we grew and made ourselves. My mother planted and harvested her own mealies. After harvesting the mealies, the woman ground the kernels between two stones. A portion of this was made into bread, while the rest was dried and stored in pots. Unlike mealies, which were sometimes in short supply, milk from our cows and goats was always plentiful.

Worksheet 27 continued

From an early age, I spent most of my free time in the veld playing and fighting with the other boys of the village. A boy who remained at home tied to his mother's apron strings was regarded as a sissy. At night, I shared my food and blanket with these same boys. I was no more than five when I became a herd-boy, looking after sheep and calves in the fields. I discovered the almost mystical attachment that the Xhosa have for cattle, not only as a source of food and wealth, but as a blessing from God and a source of happiness. It was in the fields that I learned how to knock birds out of the sky with a slingshot, to gather wild honey and fruits and edible roots, to drink warm, sweet milk straight from the udder of a cow, to swim in the clear, cold streams, and to catch fish with twine and sharpened bits of wire. I learned to stick-fight – essential knowledge to any rural African boy – and became adept at its various techniques, parrying blows, feinting in one direction, striking in another, breaking away from an opponent with quick footwork. From these days I date my love of the veld, of open spaces, the simple beauties of nature, the clean line of the horizon.

Worksheet 28

Fact, fiction and opinion

Fact	Fiction

Opinion

Worksheet 29

Fact, fiction and opinion

Nelson Mandela was born on the 18th July 1918.	Nelson Mandela was born on the 18th July 1998.
He had two names, Nelson and Rolihlahla.	He had three names, Nelson, Gadla and Rolihlahla.
Nelson Mandela's Xhosa name means, 'stirring up trouble'.	Nelson Mandela's Xhosa name means 'justice'.
It was fashionable to have a European name, preferably a heroic one.	Nelson was fascinated by tales told around the camp fire by the elders, and this led to him want to fight for his people's freedom.
His mother had three sons.	His mother had three daughters.
Nelson Mandela's father was a wealthy chief.	As a child, Nelson stole mealie cobs from the maize fields, when hungry.
As a child, Nelson Mandela only did jobs fit for a Chief's son.	As a child Nelson herded sheep and cattle.
Nelson's school textbooks were full of information about black heroes.	Nelson was shocked when history books described only white heroes.
Nelson Mandela wore his father's old clothes.	Nelson Mandela wore Chief's clothes from his early years at school.

Worksheet 30

Facts about me

Name ....

Date of birth ....

Where I was born ....

Hair colour ....

Eye colour ....

Brothers/sisters ....

....

School history ....

....

....

Childhood memories ....

....

....

....

Likes .... Dislikes ....

....

....

....

Ambitions in life including what I want to be when I grow up ....

....

....

....

Other interesting facts about me ....

....

Worksheet 31

From Nelson Mandela's autobiography, *Long Walk to Freedom* (Extract 2)

Usually the boys played among themselves, but we sometimes allowed our sisters to join us. Boys and girls would play games like ndize (hide-and-seek) and icekwa (touch and run). But the game I most enjoyed playing with the girls was what we called khetha, or choose-the-one-you-like. This was not so much an organised game, but a spur-of-the-moment sport that took place when we accosted a group of girls our own age and demanded that each select the boy she loved. Our rules dictated that the girl's choice be respected and once she had chosen her favourite, she was free to continue on her journey escorted by the lucky boy she loved. But the girls were far cleverer than us and would often confer among themselves and choose one boy, usually the plainest fellow, and then tease him all the way home.

The most popular game for boys was thinti, and like most boys' games it was a youthful approximation of war. Two sticks, used as targets, would be driven firmly into the ground in an upright position about one hundred feet apart. The goal of the game was for each team to hurl sticks at the opposing target and knock it down.

Worksheet 31 continued

We each defended our own target and attempted to prevent the other side from retrieving the sticks that had been thrown. As we grew older, we organised matches against boys from neighbouring villages, and those who distinguished themselves in these battles were greatly admired.

After games such as these, I would return to my mother's kraal where she was preparing supper. Whereas my father once told stories of historic battles and heroic Xhosa warriors, my mother would enchant us with Xhosa legends and fables that had come down from numberless generations. These tales stimulated my childish imagination, and usually contained some moral lesson. I recall one story my mother told us about a traveller who was approached by an old woman with terrible cataracts on her eyes. The woman asked the traveller for help, and the man averted his eyes. Then another man came along and was approached by the old woman. She asked him to clean her eyes, and even though he found the task unpleasant, he did as she asked. Then, miraculously, the scales fell from the old woman's eyes and she became young and beautiful. The man married her and became wealthy. It is a simple tale, but its message is an enduring one: virtue and generosity will be rewarded in ways that one cannot know.

Worksheet 31 *continued*

On the first day of school, my teacher gave each of us an English name and said that from then on that was the name we would answer to in school. This was the custom among Africans in those days and was undoubtedly due to the British bias of our education.

That day the teacher told me that my new name was Nelson. Why this particular name was bestowed on me I have no idea. Perhaps it had something to do with the great British sea captain Lord Nelson, but that would only be a guess.

Worksheet 32

Glossary

kraal	village of huts enclosed by a fence
mealie	maize
rondavel	hut
ochre	mineral of clay and hydrated ferric oxide used as pigment (dye)
sorghum	a cereal
veld	open country, neither cultivated nor true forest
ndize	a game of hide-and-seek
icekwa	a game of touch and run ('it')
khetha	a game of choose-the-one-you-like
thinti	war games
amasi	fermented milk
calabash	gourd whose shell is used for holding liquid

References

Benson, Mary (1995) 'A Desire to Serve the People' in *Five Minute Stories*, ed. Sophie Jowett, Scholastic Collections, Scholastic.

Brown, Margot (ed.)(1996) *Our World, Our Rights*, Amnesty International UK.

Castle, Caroline (2000) *For Every Child*, Hutchinson Books in association with UNICEF.

Cole, Babette (1991) *Hurrah for Ethelyn,* Heinemann.

Mandela, Nelson (1998) *Long Walk to Freedom*, Little Brown and Co.

Meredith, Martin (1997) *Nelson Mandela: A Biography*, Penguin.

Peace Child International (1988) quotation from Liam O'Neill in *Stand Up for Your Rights*, Two-Can Publishing.

Pogrund, Benjamin (1991) *Nelson Mandela: The South African leader who was imprisoned for twenty-seven years for fighting against apartheid*, Exley Publications.

Save the Children in association with UNICEF/UK (1990) *It's Our Right*.

Velthuijs, Max (1988) *Frog and the Stranger*, Andersen Press.

Chapter 5
Global Citizenship and Geography

This chapter aims to help you teach Geography in a way that promotes Global Citizenship. The first part of the chapter is very general, and contains much of relevance to People and Place in Environmental Studies in Scotland and Geography in Wales. The second part relates specifically to the English QCA Geography schemes of work.

Traditionally, Geography has had strong links with issues of Global Citizenship, because of its potential to help children interpret their environment and understand the world around them. An approach to Geography which promotes Global Citizenship is important for the following reasons.

- It encourages an all-round view of places. Some children may have negative perceptions of places, both within the UK and in distant localities. This has often been gained through one-sided media coverage, which does not always give the reasons behind particular situations.

- It encourages a questioning approach to information. It is important for children to realise that everything is written from a particular viewpoint and tends to be biased in some way.

- It challenges stereotypes and prejudiced views. The things children see when they look at a particular photograph might be different from the things you see. For example, in showing a picture of rural life in a distant locality they may register the lack of shoes or some animal dung, rather than the thriving market that you see. It is important to avoid this leading to prejudiced views or feelings of superiority.

- It is possible to bring a global dimension to all aspects of Geography. There are an infinite number of links and similarities between people's lives around the globe.

- It can link different aspects of the curriculum. Stephen Scoffham (2000) suggests the following ideas for linking Geography, environmental education and active citizenship within the local community:
  - go on field trips to field work or environmental centres
  - set up a lunchtime or after-school environment club (external organisations can be involved)
  - enter an award scheme or competition such as Eco-Schools
  - undertake practical environmental projects either as a study day or as part of a residential school trip
  - take part in seasonal events such as Riverwatch, Industry Week, Environmental Week (organised each May by the Civic Trust), or Geography Action Week (organised by the Geographical Association each autumn).

Many of the in-service activities in Chapter 2 will stimulate discussion, which will be helpful in the teaching of Geography. These activities promote the exploration of questions such as teaching about contentious issues, presenting positive images, detecting bias, using artefacts, and inviting visitors into school.

Maps

An excellent starting point for promoting Global Citizenship through Geography is to examine the school's world maps.

The map of the world which you may remember from your own school days, and which is still commonly seen, is the Mercator Projection. This shows Europe as the centre of the world, and very large compared with the equatorial regions. It was drawn in the Netherlands by Gerhard Mercator in the 16th century for use in exploration. It is perhaps not surprising then, that Europe is so dominant – only surprising that such a clear example of Euro-centricity and bias should have been used for so long. Here is a quick exercise you might find interesting. Below are two different projections of the world: how do they strike you?

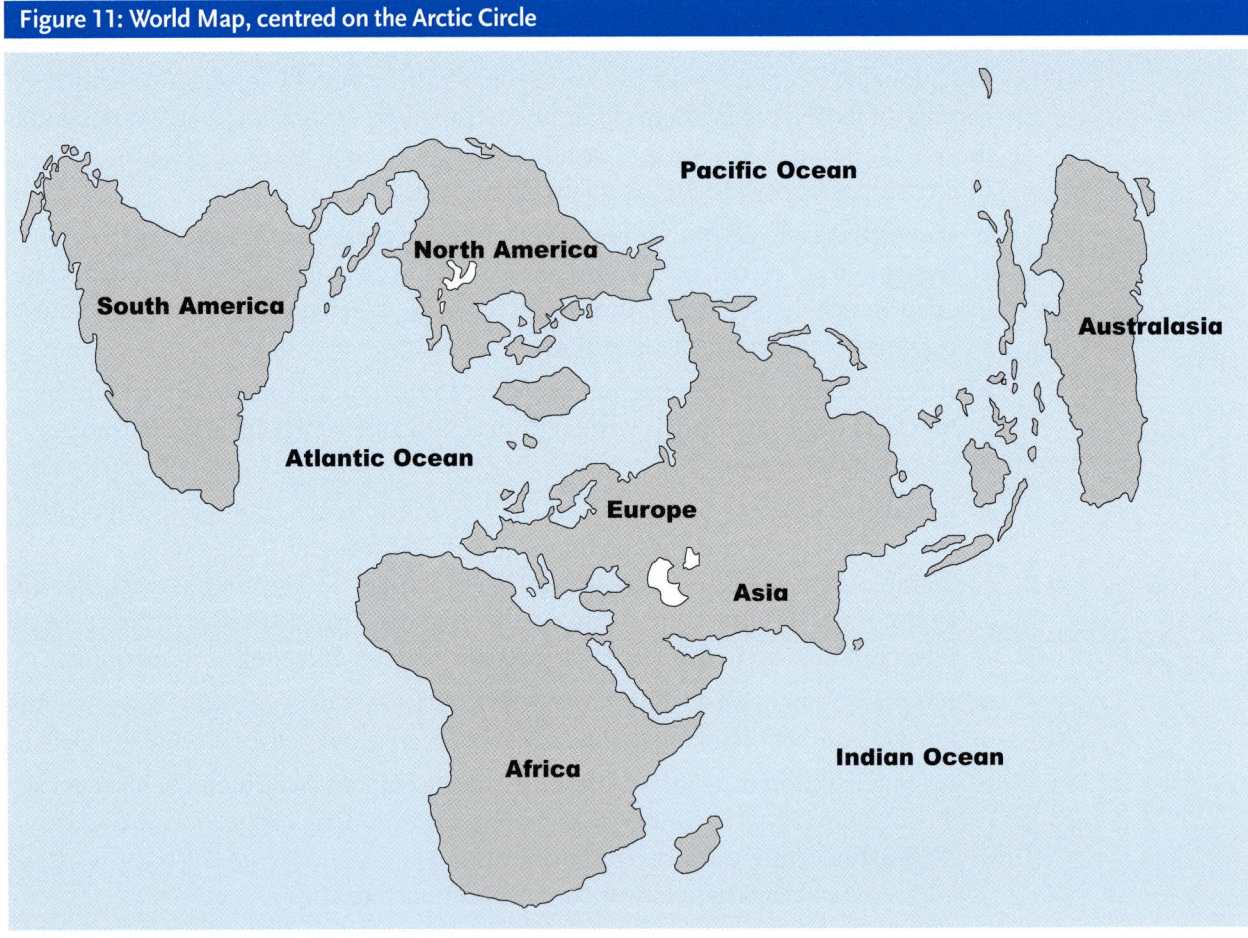

Figure 11: World Map, centred on the Arctic Circle

Taken from **Mapping Our World** (Oxfam, 2000)

Figure 12: Peters Projection, oriented with east at the top

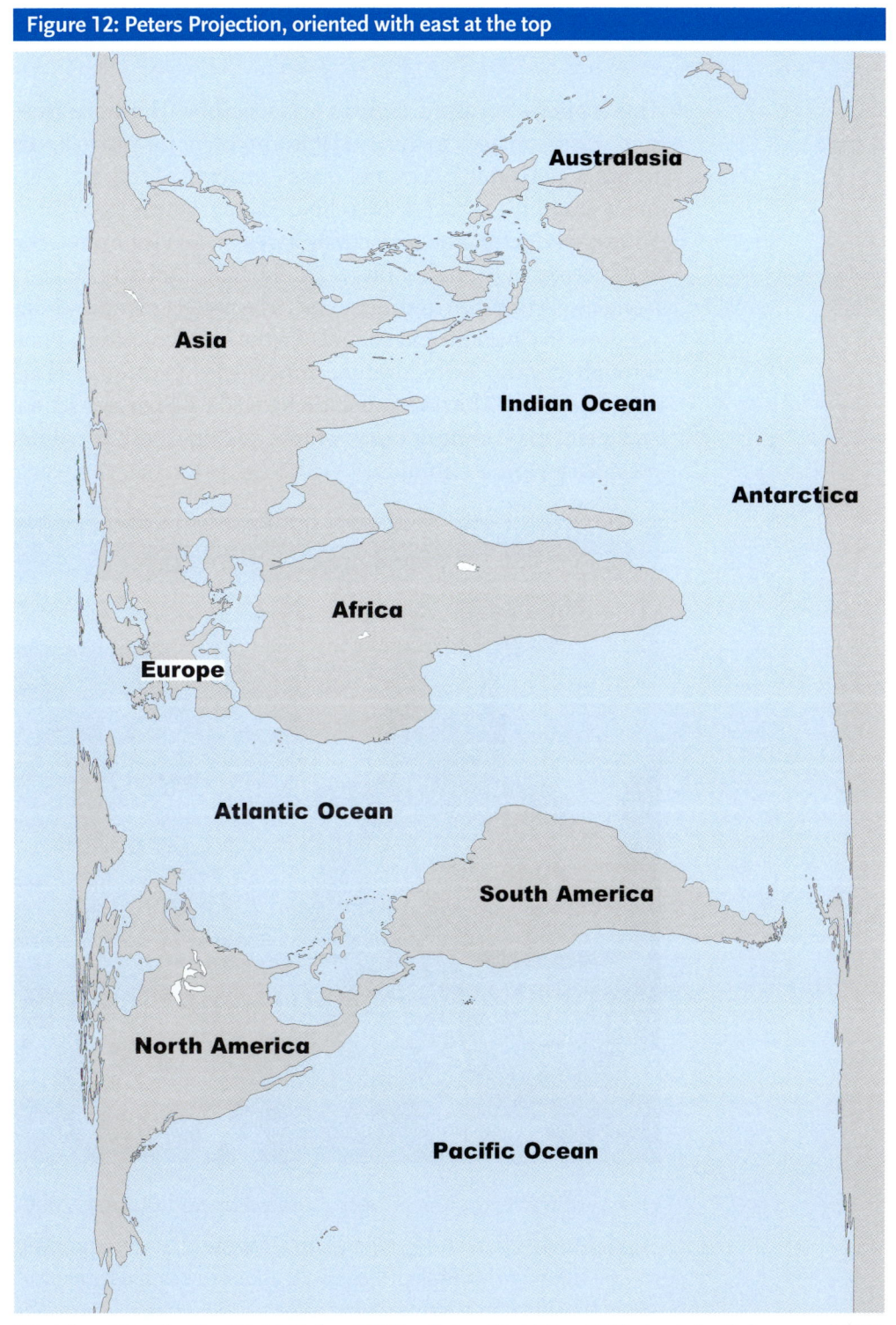

Taken from **Mapping Our World** (Oxfam, 2000)   Peters World Map © Akademische Verlagsanstalt 2002

Both these maps are equally valid, but they are centred on different places, and make different compromises in order to show the globe – a three-dimensional object – on a two-dimensional piece of paper. The first is centred on the Arctic Circle. The second, is a Peters Projection 'orientated' with east at the top. This orientation was used in Medieval times by European mapmakers who thought that the centre of Christianity (to the east of the UK) was the most important place in the world. They therefore put the east at the top of the map. Map projections which offer a fairly balanced view of the world are the Peters Projection, where countries are shown according to exact land mass, and the Ekhert IV, which is also an equal-area projection.

School linking

This is often seen as the domain of Geography. There are great advantages, but also some disadvantages in this, and it is important for you to be aware of all the issues before undertaking it. Chapter 6 has contacts and resources to help you. There are many examples of successful school linking. One is from Cheshire Development Education Centre. The project was based on an idea from Geography Action Week, and was part of the millennium 'On the Line' initiative, which linked countries along the Greenwich Meridian Line. The project compared the views from school windows in Cheshire and several 'On the Line' countries. Photos were taken through the school windows and annotated with comments and concerns about the issues depicted. They were then exchanged with partner schools. Both the schools and their local communities were involved. In Cheshire, some Ghanaian visitors provided an initial stimulus.

Photo 4: Miso'shi Fiadogbe-Procter drumming with friends at a school in Cheshire (by Heather Swainston)

Heather Swainston, the project coordinator said (Young, 2000):

> It's vital that children have an awareness, understanding and respect for the wider world. This project is all about making connections and giving children lifeskills for a global world.

Here are some comments from teachers involved:

> Quite a few of the children showed talents and skills previously untapped, e.g. dance and drumming.

> The work clarified some of the stereotyped images our children had of Ghana.

School twinning and sponsoring children in the Majority World are also often seen as the remit of Geography. As with school linking, careful thought and planning is required for these initiatives to be successful.

Teaching about distant localities

The issues raised in Activities 3, 4 and 5 on 'presenting positive images', in Chapter 2, are very relevant when teaching about distant localities. In order to help frame questions about a locality, here are some useful enquiry questions from Brownlie (1995:16). They can be used for any locality and in a number of subject areas in addition to Geography.

- Where is this place?
- What does it look like?
- What is this place like?
- What made it like that?
- What is it like to live there?
- How do people use and care for the environment?
- What links does it have with other places?
- What would it feel like to be in this place?
- How is this place changing?
- What are the issues affecting people who live there?
- What are the views of the people who live there?
- Who decides what should happen in this place?
- Why is this place special?

More helpful guidance comes in the 'Development Compass Rose' developed by Birmingham Development Education Centre. It provides a framework for asking a range of questions about development issues in any locality. For further information and explanation, see *Development Compass Rose* (1995) by Birmingham DEC.

QCA Geography schemes of work

This part of the chapter looks at how Global Citizenship can be incorporated into the QCA Geography schemes of work. It is laid out in tables that are designed to be used alongside the schemes of work. A number of the units have been chosen, those which raise specific issues of Global Citizenship. The QCA learning objectives for these have been listed. Next to these are Global Citizenship (GC) learning outcomes which could be gained through doing the unit, and a list of points to note, which highlight issues and give guidance on teaching in a way that promotes Global Citizenship. References are also made to other parts of the Handbook which will provide further useful information.

Although this part of the chapter has been written to be used in conjunction with the QCA schemes of work, many of the points raised are relevant to the Welsh curriculum and to the study of People and Place in Scotland.

Unit 1 Around our school – the local area

QCA learning objectives	GC learning outcomes	GC points to note
Where do I live?	■ begin to value resources	■ Discuss the environmental impact of different types of travel. Look at different points of view.
Where do other pupils live?	■ understand our impact on the environment ■ have concern for the wider environment ■ have a willingness to care for the environment ■ have an awareness that our actions have consequences	■ Discuss the factors which add to the quality of the environment, and what children can do to maintain a 'nice' and transform a 'nasty' place. ■ Talk about the rights and responsibilities we all have for the local area. ■ For contacts and resources to help with environmental issues, see Chapter 6.
What are our immediate surroundings like?	■ awareness of past and future	■ Involve the local community: ask a local resident to come and talk to the pupils about how the area has changed in their lifetime.
Are there any changes taking place in our area?	■ develop an enquiring mind	■ See page 161 for locality study enquiry questions.

Unit 5 Where in the world is Barnaby Bear?

QCA learning objectives	GC learning outcomes	GC points to note
Where has Barnaby Bear travelled to this week or month?	■ look at different viewpoints ■ make links between our lives and the lives of others ■ tact and diplomacy involving/including society and others ■ interest and concern for others in wider sphere	■ In asking pupils how 'other places' may be different from their own locality, encourage pupils to look for similarities in terms of basic human needs: shelter, food, clothing. Observe differences, for instance in use of housing materials dependent on local availability and appropriateness for the climate. (See Chapter 2, activity 3, page 20 for ways to avoid stereotyping.)

Continued overleaf

Unit 5 Where in the world is Barnaby Bear? continued

QCA learning objectives	GC learning outcomes	GC points to note

Can we find these places on a map?	As above, plus:
	■ begin to state an opinion based on evidence
		■ Maps: Peters and Ekhert IV map projections are equal-area projections, i.e. they are more realistic and balanced in their portrayal of the different continents than projections such as Mercator. (See 'maps' page 158).
		
		■ Be sure that any displays of Barnaby's destinations show an all-round view of the countries: you may need to add particular postcards or photographs to show different aspects of the countries visited (e.g. countryside, city area, areas of greater and lesser affluence). One postcard of the Costa del Sol to depict Spain is clearly not the whole story. (See Chapter 2, pages 20–22, Activities 3 and 4.)
		
		■ If asking children to label photographs and postcards 'like/don't like', as suggested in this unit, try asking pupils to say what they like or do not like about their own locality before moving on to the unknown locality. There are probably things about all areas that we like and don't like! Also, consider the following:
		  – What are the pupils going to base their judgements on? Will the range of pictures available enable them to give a reasoned opinion?
		  – Could the exercise lead to pupils making negative statements about the places? If so, how will you ensure any stereotyped views are not reinforced? (See Chapter 2, pages 20–23, Activities 3, 4 and 5.)

What will it be like when Barnaby is there?	As above	■ In using artefacts from different countries some, as suggested, may be coins, newspapers etc., but be aware that some may need more sensitive handling, e.g. religious artefacts. (See Chapter 2, page 22, Activity 4.) ■ In encouraging pupils to look for similarities and differences between 'other countries and their own', focus on a named place, on common links, and avoid generalisations about places to help ensure that comparisons do not lead to negativity and prejudiced views. (See Chapter 2, page 20, Activity 3.)
How did Barnaby travel to these places?	As above, plus: ■ awareness of rich and poor ■ willingness to learn from the experiences of others ■ begin to value resources ■ awareness that our actions have consequences	■ Think about the implications for sustainable development of various types of transport, e.g. which are the most polluting? which are the most environmentally friendly? This could also link with Maths, e.g. the use of statistics on pollution. ■ Think about how appropriate different types of transport are: donkeys may seem 'old fashioned' or low-tech, but in certain circumstances they are simply the best, as well as the most affordable, form of transport.

Unit 7 Weather around the world

QCA learning objectives	GC learning outcomes	GC points to note
What is the place like? **How similar is it to, and how different from, our locality?**	■ understand the nature of prejudice and ways to combat it ■ understand the relationship between people and the environment ■ detect bias, opinion and stereotypes ■ empathy towards others globally	■ In encouraging pupils to find out about different countries, ensure that they are beginning to recognise bias, and developing critical thinking skills. (See 'Bias Alert!', Chapter 2, page 23, Activity 5.) ■ For a locality study, the questions on page 161 can be very useful. ■ In asking pupils to find out about 'life in the chosen locality', if possible focus on a named family and their everyday lives. This will help pupils relate to them as individuals. Help pupils to gain as balanced a view as possible about the lives of other people and discourage them from making value judgements about others. ■ In asking pupils to look at similarities and differences between their own locality and lifestyle and those in other places, ensure stereotypes are not reinforced. (See Chapter 2, page 20, Activity 3.)
What will the weather be like? **How will it affect what we do?** This could be extended to looking at why the extremes of weather affect countries differently, depending on whether they are 'rich' or 'poor'. The GC learning outcomes and points to note are related to this.	■ causes and effects of inequality ■ recognise and start to challenge unfairness ■ empathy towards others globally	■ The main reason for the difference in effect of extreme weather conditions on different localities is poverty. Poverty causes a lack of sound infrastructure – poorly maintained roads and inadequate funds available for emergency purposes. Another effect is deforestation, with wood needed for fuel and land required for cultivation. Deforestation leads to soil erosion and thus to increased seriousness in the effects of droughts and floods.

Unit 8 Improving the environment

QCA learning objectives	GC learning outcomes	GC points to note
What is the environment like in school?	■ sense of responsibility for the environment and the use of resources	■ In discussing environmental problems in and around the school, ensure that pupils understand what they can do to improve the situation.
What do we throw away in the classroom? How could it be reduced? **How much do we throw away in the school grounds? How could it be reduced?**	■ awareness of finite resources ■ our potential to change things ■ belief that things can be better and that individuals can make a difference	■ Go further than simply discussing what types of things can be recycled: – question why so much is wasted, and how this can be decreased, i.e. refuse, reduce, reuse, recycle, restore, respect. – do a school sustainable development audit and produce a school policy – lobby the local council to provide more glass, paper, tin and plastic banks for everyone's use in your local area. (See Chapter 6 for recycling contacts.)

Unit 10 A village in India

QCA learning objectives	GC learning outcomes	GC points to note
How is Chembakolli connected to other places? What do we think it will be like there?	■ nature of prejudice and ways to combat it ■ detect bias, opinion and stereotypes ■ empathy towards others globally ■ growing interest in world events ■ growing respect for difference and diversity	■ When you ask pupils what they think India or Chembakolli is like (places they may not have visited), their answers may reveal misconceptions. It is important that you are able to combat stereotyped or prejudiced views they may hold. (See Chapter 2, page 20, Activity 3.) The enquiry questions on page 161 are useful starting points in learning about distant localities. ■ Inviting a visitor to the school who has been to India or is from India could help to give pupils an insight into the country. (There may also be pupils who can do this.)

What are the homes of the children in Chembakolli like?
 	
What is the school in Chembakolli like?
 	
What is the main type of work in Chembakolli?
 	
How do people sell and trade goods in Chembakolli?
 	
What are the main similarities and differences between our locality and Chembakolli?
	■ understanding of the relationship between people and the environment; there is also the possibility of bringing the following into discussions on trading goods:
	  – trade between countries
	  – Fair Trade
		■ Each of these learning objectives suggest making comparisons between Chembakolli and the locality of the pupils. Ensure such activities do not lead to unfavourable comparisons, generalisations and prejudice. Chembakolli is a rural village in India, different in many ways from rural villages in the UK, let alone a city. (See Chapter 2, pages 20–23, Activities 3, 4 and 5, for ideas on positive imaging.)
		■ In looking at main types of work in Chembakolli, focus on the similarities with village life in the UK, e.g. washing, plant cultivation, etc.
		■ Find resources depicting life in other parts of India, including urban areas where life would be different from that in Chembakolli, as it is between urban and rural areas in the UK. Using more than one resource will give a more representative view of life in India than that gained by looking only at Chembakolli.

Unit 11 Water

QCA learning objectives	GC learning outcomes	GC points to note
Who uses water? What do they use it for?	■ recognise and start to challenge unfairness ■ empathy towards others locally and globally ■ sense of responsibility for the environment and the use of resources ■ belief that things can be better and that individuals can make a difference	■ Go further than discussing the issue of wasting water: talk about ways of reducing waste, and how everyone can do something to make a difference. Perhaps pupils could survey their own water usage, leading to ideas for reduction. You could start with a thought-provoking question followed by a simple experiment, e.g. how little water could it take to clean your teeth?

Continued overleaf

Unit 11 Water continued

QCA learning objectives	GC learning outcomes	GC points to note
Is all water usable? **How can water be made usable?**	As above	■ This unit encourages children to know about 'times when people did not have clean water'. However, globally speaking, at present: – 40 per cent of the Earth's population does not have access to clean water – 80 per cent of the disease in Majority World countries is because of poor drinking water and sanitation (New Internationalist 2000) – although we have the means to provide clean water to 95 per cent of the world's population by 2035, whether or not this happens is a matter of political will. Currently, '… half the world doesn't have sanitation equal to Ancient Rome' (Gleick 1999).
Who owns water? **Who pays for water?** **What jobs are involved in providing our water?**	■ relationship between people and the environment ■ growing interest in world events	■ Several aid agencies are involved with water provision, e.g. Wateraid and Oxfam. Oxfam's work here is mainly in emergencies, either clearing out wells where there has been flooding, or digging boreholes in refugee camps and treating surface water so that it is clean to drink. A special bucket has also been developed which is used widely in emergencies. It holds 14 litres, and has a clip-on top with a hole and cap to ensure the water inside is kept clean.

Unit 16 What's in the news?

QCA learning objectives	GC learning outcomes	GC points to note
What is in the local or national newspapers today? **Where is this place?** **What is happening there?**	■ detect bias, opinion and stereotypes ■ empathy towards others locally	■ Encourage pupils to be sensitive in the use of images. (See Chapter 2, page 20, Activity 3).
What is in the local, national or international news today? **Where are these places?** **What is happening there? Why?**	As above, plus: ■ find and select evidence ■ recognise and start to challenge unfairness ■ empathy towards others locally and globally ■ growing interest in world events ■ sense of justice	■ Global Express, for 8–13 year olds (see Chapter 6 for details) is an excellent source of background information on current world affairs. It explains the reasons behind the issues, and therefore events can be put in context. ■ Natural disasters occur everywhere in the world: it is their impact on the local community that has different effects. Making connections between international and local situations can help pupils understand events. For instance, the effects of local flooding can be used as a starting point in trying to look at flooding elsewhere. Use local and international photographs whenever possible. ■ Find specific details about places that are affected by severe weather (or disasters) – it is not likely to be the entire country or continent.

Continued overleaf

Unit 16 What's in the news? continued

QCA learning objectives	GC learning outcomes	GC points to note
What is happening in our local area?	■ understand the causes of conflict ■ assess different viewpoints ■ begin to present a reasoned case ■ compromise	■ If a news bulletin is produced about a local issue, send it to the local paper. This will increase the pupils' self-esteem and encourage them to feel that their views are important in the community.
What is in the radio traffic news today?	■ sense of responsibility for the environment and the use of resources	■ There is growing interest in 'walk to school' and other school travel initiatives. (See *A Safer Journey to School* (1999) in Chapter 6.)
What is happening in our local area? **How and why is the place changing?** **How will people in the community respond?**	■ belief that things can be better and that individuals can make a difference	■ The topic would be more realistic if the radio report produced was featured on a local radio station.

Unit 17 Global eye

This unit presents the opportunity to investigate some important issues related to sight. However, it seems rather disjointed in its line of questioning, ranging from recycling at home to describing the African countryside. It is an optional unit, and if it is to be included, care needs to be taken to avoid pupils gaining the impression that people in African countries rely purely on charity handouts from the Minority World in order to obtain spectacles.

QCA learning objectives	GC learning outcomes	GC points to note
Why are eyes important? **What is it like not to be able to see?**	■ look at different viewpoints ■ empathise with the needs of others ■ make links between our lives and the lives of others	■ For further information about visual impairment see contacts in Chapter 6. ■ Consider the reasons for sight loss: this can be different in different parts of the world. Cataracts are the most common cause of blindness in Majority World countries, and although they are very easy to remove, not everyone has access to treatment.
What do we recycle at home?	■ tact and diplomacy involving/including society and others ■ begin to value resources ■ awareness that our actions have consequences	■ Ask pupils about their family's recycling practices at home, and discuss what more, if anything, could be done. Individual pledges could be made, with each pupil deciding on what, realistically, they will do around the home and school to reduce waste. ■ For contacts and resources on recycling, waste reduction and conservation, e.g. Wastewatch, see Chapter 6.

Continued overleaf

Unit 17 Global eye continued

QCA learning objectives	GC learning outcomes	GC points to note
What is the African countryside like? **How do children in African countries get spectacles?**	■ awareness of rich and poor ■ greater awareness of similarities and differences between people ■ develop an enquiring mind ■ interest and concern for others in wider sphere ■ sense of personal indignation ■ willingness to participate	■ Provide a range of images of each of the African countries referred to, showing the diversity of African landscapes and settlements. In asking pupils to illustrate how their local area differs from the African areas depicted, focus also on similarities, e.g. common human needs such as shelter and food, and familiar things like trees and places to play. Comparisons can only be realistically made if they match like with like: compare large towns in the UK with large towns in African countries, e.g. Nairobi and Accra. Use pictures of the UK countryside, e.g. the Yorkshire Dales, Brecon Beacons or Scottish Highlands if rural landscapes are to be compared. (See Chapter 2, pages 20–23, Activities 3, 4 and 5, on positive imaging.) ■ In asking pupils how people in an African country can obtain spectacles, point out that there are options in African countries, but that not every area of each country is served equally, and also that the cost of spectacles is too great for many families. This is important to give context to the work of charity organisations (both local and from overseas, e.g. Sightsavers) working in this field. ■ See Chapter 6 for contacts for further information.

Unit 20 Local traffic – an environmental issue

QCA learning objectives	GC learning outcomes	GC points to note
What are the issues involved in constructing the bypass?	■ understand the causes and impact of conflict ■ assess different viewpoints ■ begin to present a reasoned case ■ sense of importance of individual worth ■ sense of responsibility for the environment and the use of resources	■ Encourage pupils to hold and give their opinions on local issues – to become active citizens. For example, pupils could write to the local paper, lobby the council, give a local radio interview, or hold a class, school or inter-school debate on the issues.
Why is the construction of the bypass an issue?	■ empathy towards others locally ■ detect bias, opinion and stereotypes ■ assess different viewpoints	■ When asking pupils to discuss how the issue is expressed by others, encourage them to spot the difference between fact and opinion, and encourage pupils to express their own views.

Continued overleaf

Unit 20 Local traffic – an environmental issue continued

QCA learning objectives	GC learning outcomes	GC points to note
What are the groups involved in the issue and what are their views?	As above	As above ■ The questionnaire survey of the main groups involved could be used as the starting point for contact with the media or council.
How might the issue be resolved?	■ strategies for tackling conflict and for the prevention of conflict prevention	■ Take pupils to a public meeting and encourage them to represent the views of the school.

Unit 22 A contrasting locality overseas – Tocuaro

QCA learning objectives	GC learning outcomes	GC points to note
Where is Tocuaro?	■ sense of the wider world ■ links and connections between different places ■ interest and concern for others in wider sphere	■ Teaching about overseas localities will lead to greater global knowledge and can lead to greater global understanding, as stated in this unit. However, unbiased and deep understanding is only likely to happen if the teacher presents an all-round picture of the locality and is able to combat any misinformed views the pupils may have. (You may find the locality study questions on page 16 helpful.) ■ In asking pupils to describe what Tocuaro might be like, ensure that they have enough information to enable them to make informed suggestions.
What is the village of Tocuaro like?	As above	■ In looking at similarities and differences between Tocuaro and their own localities, encourage pupils to look for things that are common to most people throughout the world, e.g. homes, food, plants.

Continued overleaf

Unit 22 A contrasting locality overseas – Tocuaro continued

QCA learning objectives	GC learning outcomes	GC points to note
What might it be like to live in Tocuaro?	As above, plus: ■ develop an enquiring mind ■ begin to state an opinion based on evidence ■ empathise with the needs of others ■ make links between our lives and the lives of others ■ value others as equal and different	■ In encouraging pupils to think about what life might be like in Tocuaro, try to give them a taste of different aspects of life in Mexico – for instance, contemporary and traditional music, art, fashion, and architecture. ■ Within the suggested history element of the unit, encourage the pupils to think about the use of available materials and appropriate technology before comparing old and new cooking utensils in Mexico and the UK. It is quite hard to get an accurate picture of the range of modern utensils available in Mexico from the photograph provided; additional photographs would be helpful. ■ Mask-making: ensure that the simplicity of the suggested art activity does not lead pupils to think that the masks made by the Horta family are unsophisticated. Ensure that the pupils are aware of the reason why the family makes these masks – put them in context. Some real masks could be brought to the lesson and their uses explained; some are supposed to be frightening! (See Chapter 2, page 22, Activity 4.) ■ When exploring the point about sustainable development and pollution, focus on similar debates in the pupils' own lives. It is necessary to go beyond looking at what 'other people' should do to stop polluting their environment.

Unit 24 Passport to the world

This unit is continuous across KS1 and KS2.

QCA learning objectives	GC learning outcomes	GC points to note
KS1 *What links do I have with other places in the world*	■ greater awareness of similarities and differences between people ■ sense of the wider world ■ links and connections between places ■ our impact on the environment ■ interest and concern for others in the wider sphere	■ If possible, use an equal-area world map, e.g. Peters or Ekhert 1V Projection, see page 158. Globes can give a more accurate representation of the Earth than two-dimensional projection. ■ In using postcards from around the world, ensure that an all-round picture of each country is shown, e.g. rural and urban scenes, contemporary and historical views. (See Chapter 2, page 22, Activity 3.) 'Our links around the world' (Chapter 3, page 45, Activity 9 and page 85, Activity 42) are activities to encourage children to begin to think about interdependence, and what it means. ■ Fair Trade could be brought into this unit: in addition to collecting a range of packaging to identify country of origin, pupils could look for items marked with the Fairtrade Foundation symbol. (See Chapter 3, pages 88–89, Activity 43.) ■ Tourism issues could also come in here. (See contacts in Chapter 6.)

Continued overleaf

Unit 24 Passport to the world continued

QCA learning objectives	GC learning outcomes	GC points to note
How are places similar to, and different from, other places?	As above	■ Note that the shapes of countries will be determined by whether they use a globe, or by which map projection the pupils use. ■ If similarities and differences are to be found between places, generalisations can be avoided by looking at a variety of pictures from any given place: just because a photograph doesn't show a park doesn't mean there isn't one in the area. In making comparisons, match like with like.
What can we find out about places from different media?	■ greater awareness of similarities and differences between people ■ interest and concern for others in the wider sphere ■ look at different viewpoints ■ develop an enquiring mind	■ Ensure that work using different media includes a critical element so that pupils can learn to tell fact from opinion. ■ As well as reading stories set in different places, it would be interesting to read a couple of stories set in the same place and to look at how the two portrayals differ. ■ In asking pupils questions such as 'What would it be like to live there?', ensure that they have enough to go on in order to make a fair judgement. (See questions for a locality study on page 161.) ■ See Chapter 3, page 45, Assembly activity 9 'Links across the globe' for an idea to encourage pupils to look for links between peoples. ■ There are some ideas of stories set in places around the world in Chapter 6, especially on page 175.
KS2 **How do we find out about places?**	■ understand the relationship between people and the environment ■ assess different viewpoints ■ empathy towards others locally and globally ■ growing interest in world events	■ Issues of responsible tourism could be included here, e.g. discussions on appropriate and unacceptable behaviour and the benefits and drawbacks of tourism to the host community. (See Chapter 6 for contacts, such as Tourism Concern.) ■ The variations in the adverse effect of weather in different places are often due to differences in wealth of countries.
What are the reasons for places being mentioned in the news?	■ depending on what is in the news, all the GC learning outcomes could potentially be covered by this question	■ Ensure that the 'why' behind events is investigated. With disasters this can often be poverty, conflict or inequality of resources distribution. Materials such as Global Express (see Chapter 6) can be helpful here.
How are places described in stories?	■ empathy towards others globally	■ See Chapter 6 for some other books suitable for use here.

Photo 5: Bhavini Algarra from Canterbury DEC helping pupils at Selling School, Kent, set up email links with schools overseas (Faversham Gazette and Times)

References

Ashmore, Bernie (2000) *Mapping our World*, Oxfam.

Brace, Steve (1996) *Chembakolli,* Actionaid.

Brownlie, Ali (1995) *Teaching About Localities: A Development Education Approach*, Oxfam.

Bunce, V., Gibbs, F., Morgan, W. and Wakefield, D. (1998) *Tocuaro: A Mexican Village*, The Geographical Association.

Development Compass Rose (1995) Birmingham DEC.

'Factfile on Water' (2000) in *New Internationalist,* 322:4.

Global Express (periodical teachers' notes) Manchester Development Education Project and the Panos Institute.

Gleick, Peter H., 'Biennial Report on Freshwater Resources 1998–99' (published by Island Press) in *The Guardian*, 31 March 1999.

QCA (1998) *Geography: A Scheme of Work for Key Stages 1 and 2*, QCA.

Scoffham, Stephen (2000) 'Environmental Education: A Question of Values' in C. Fisher and T. Binns (eds) *Issues in Geography Teaching*, Routledge.

Young, Mary (2000) 'The Future's so Bright', in *Primary Geographer,* 40:22–23, Geographical Association.

Chapter 6
Resources and contacts

The books, resources, games and websites listed in this chapter provide ideas and activities which explore issues of Global Citizenship. We have categorised them into the five Global Citizenship themes, but many cover several or all of them. The books marked with an asterisk can be obtained through the *Oxfam Education Resources for Schools* catalogue. For free catalogues and Global Citizenship teachers' guides please contact Oxfam Supporter Information Department on 01865 312610, or email **oxfam@oxfam.org.uk**, or visit our website: **www.oxfam.org.uk/coolplanet**.

Children's books

The following is a selection of picture books and non-fiction texts. Many of the books are recent publications; others are older, but remain invaluable. Some are available in big book format. Many other books not listed here, for instance traditional stories, are nevertheless useful in explaining issues. 'The Three Billy Goats Gruff', for example, clearly centres on territorial bullying.

Social justice and equity

	Foundation Stage, Pre 5/Early Years	KS1/P1–3	KS2/P4–7
Fiction	*Bootsie Barker Bites* (1992) Barbara Bottner Penguin *Clown* (1995) Quentin Blake Jonathan Cape *I like it when* (1997) Mary Murphy Methuen Children's Books and Mammoth *I'm Sorry* (2000) Sam McBratney Harper Collins *Little Rabbit Foo Foo* (1990) Michael Rosen Walker Books *Poems about you and me* (1998) Compiled by Brian Moses (poetry) Wayland	*Aldo* (1993) John Burningham Red Fox *Frog is a Hero* (1995) Max Velthuijs Andersen Press *Hurrah for Ethelyn* (1991) Babette Cole Mammoth *It's always me they're after* (1999) Ann De Bode and Rien Broere Evans *Oops* (1996) Colin McNaughton Andersen Press Ltd *The Rainbow Fish* (1992) Marcus Pfister North South Books Inc. *Sanji and the Baker* (1993) Robin Tzannes Oxford University Press	*Amazing Grace* (1991) Mary Hoffman Frances Lincoln *The Legend of Freedom Hill* (2000) Linda Jacobs Altman Lee and Low Books *Mamo on the Mountain* (1994) Jane Kurtz Puffin Books *Nobody Rides the Unicorn* (1999) Adrian Mitchell Picture Corgi Books *Wicked World* (2000) Benjamin Zephaniah (poetry) Puffin Books *The Wild Washerwomen* (1979) John Yeoman Hamish Hamilton
Non-fiction		*Play on the Line* (2000)* Nikki Daly and Don Harrison Humanities Education Centre	*For Every Child* (2000) Caroline Castle Hutchinson Books in association with UNICEF *The Life of Stephen Lawrence* (2001)* V.A. Wilkins Tamarind

Global Citizenship: The Handbook for Primary Teaching

Globalisation and interdependence

	Foundation Stage, Pre 5/Early Years	KS1/P1–3	KS2/P4–7
Fiction	*Bear about town* (2000) Stella Blackstone Bearfoot Books *Handa's Surprise* (1994) Eileen Browne Walker Books *Hug* (2000) Jez Alborough Walker Books *Over in the Grasslands* (1999) Anna Wilson and Alison Bartlett Macmillan *Skip across the Ocean* (1995)* Collected by Floella Benjamin (rhymes) Frances Lincoln	*A Balloon for Grandad* (1988) Nigel Gray Orchard Books *A Caribbean Dozen* (1994)* John Agardt and Grace Nichols (eds) (poetry) Walker Books *The Gigantic Turnip* (1998) Aleksei Tolstoy Barefoot Books *The Leopard's Drum* (1995) Jessica Souhami Frances Lincoln *The Little Boat* (1995) Kathy Henderson Walker Books *Rainbow Bird* (1993) Eric Maddern Frances Lincoln *So Much* (1994) Trish Cooke Walker Books *The Wonderful Journey* (1999) Paul Geraghty Red Fox	*The Boy Who Sailed with Columbus* (1991) Michael Foreman Pavilion Books *The Day of Ahmed's Secret* (1997) Florence Parry Heide Puffin *South and North, East and West* (1992)* Michael Rosen (ed.) Walker Books *Tibet through the Red Box* (1998) Peter Sis Allen & Unwin *The Time of the Lion* (1998) Caroline Pitcher Frances Lincoln *The Way of the Birds* (1996) Meme McDonald Allen & Unwin *When Jessie Came Across the Sea* (1999) Amy Hest Walker Books
Non-fiction		*Nii Kwei's Day* (2001)* Francis Provencal and Catherine McNamara Frances Lincoln *Shompa Lives in India* (1999)* Jean Harrison Christian Aid	*Global Express* (rapid response bulletin to major items in the news) Manchester Development Education Project/PANOS *The People of St Lucia* (1998)* *The Landscape of St Lucia* (1998)* Alison Brownlie Wayland

Appreciation of diversity

	Foundation Stage, Pre 5/Early Years	KS1/P1–3	KS2/P4–7
Fiction	*Floppy* (1999) Guido Van Genechten Mantra Publishing Ltd *Hungry! Hungry! Hungry!* (2000) Malachy Doyle Andersen Press *The Perfect Little Monster* (2000) Judy Hindley Walker Books *Skip across the Ocean* (1995)* Collected by Floella Benjamin (rhymes) Frances Lincoln *Susan Laughs* (1999) Jean Willis Andersen Press	*Boris, The Beetle who Wouldn't Stay Down* (2000) Hiawyn Oram Andersen Press *Frog and the Stranger* (1988) Max Velthuijs Andersen Press *Herb, The Vegetarian Dragon* (1999) Jules Bass Barefoot Books *Hue Boy* (1992) Rita Phillips Mitchell Victor Gollancz *Lily's Secret* (1994) Miko Imai Walker Books *Prince Cinders* (1987) Babette Cole Hamish Hamilton *Something Else* (1994) Kathryn Cave Viking *Some Things are Scary* (2000) Florence Parry Heide Walker Books *Three Cheers for Tacky* (1996) Helen Lester Macmillan Children's Books	*Fly, Bessie, Fly* (1998) Lynn Joseph Simon Schuster Books *How the World Began and Other Stories of Creation* (1996) Andrew Matthews Macdonald Young Books *Panda's Puzzle* (1977) Michael Foreman Hamish Hamilton *Six Perfectly Different Pigs* (1993) Adrienne Geoghegan Hazar Publishing Ltd *The Visitors who Came to Stay* (1984) Annalena McAfee Hamish Hamilton *Weslandia* (2000) Paul Fleischman Walker Books
Non-fiction		*W is for World* (1998)* Kathryn Cave Francis Lincoln Ltd *Wake up, World!* (1999)* Beatrice Hollyer Frances Lincoln in association with Oxfam	*For Every Racism* (1999) Jagdish Gundara and Roger Hewitt Evans Brothers *I Have a Dream* (1997) Dr Martin Luther King Scholastic Press, NY *Voices from Eritrea* (1991) Rachel Warner (ed.) Minority Rights Group

Sustainable development

	Foundation Stage, Pre 5/Early Years	KS1/P1–3	KS2/P4–7
Fiction	*Oi! Get off our Train* (1989) John Burningham Cape *Splash!* (1999) Flora McDonnell Walker Books *What's This?* (2000) Caroline Mockford Barefoot Books *Where the Forest Meets the Sea* (1989) Jeannie Baker Walker Books *Window* (1991) Jeannie Baker Red Fox	*After the Storm* (1992) Nick Butterworth Harper Collins *Dear Greenpeace* (1991) Simon James Walker Books *Dinosaurs and all that Rubbish* (1972) Michael Foreman Hamish Hamilton *Growing Good* (1999) Bernard Ashley Bloomsbury Children's Books *Kofi and the Butterflies* (1995) Sandra Horn Tamarind *The Scarecrow's Hat* (2000) Ken Brown Andersen Press Ltd *The Storm* (2000) Kathy Henderson Walker Books *The Wonder Thing* (1995) Libby Hathorn Viking *The Lorax* (1988) Dr Seuss Picture Lions	*Brother, Eagle, Sister, Sky* (1991) Susan Jeffers Puffin Books *Fly, Grandad's Prayers of the Earth* (1999) Douglas Wood Walker Books *One World* (1990) Michael Foreman Andersen Press *The People who Hugged The Trees* (1990) Adapted by Deborah Lee Rose Roberts Rinehart Inc. *The Rainbow Bear* (2000) Michael Morpugo Picture Corgi Books *The Tower to the Sun* (1996) Colin Thompson Julia Mackae Books
Non-fiction		*One Child, One Seed* (2002)* Kathryn Cave Frances Lincoln in association with Oxfam	*Keeping Water Clean* (1997) Ewan McLeish Wayland *Stand up for your Rights* (2001)* Peace Child International Two-Can Publishing

Peace and conflict resolution

	Foundation Stage, Pre 5/Early Years	KS1/P1–3	KS2/P4–7
Fiction	*Eat your Dinner* (1994) Virginia Miller Walker Books	*Dogger* (1977) Shirley Hughes Red Fox	*Catkin* (1994) Antonia Barber Walker Books
	Little Dragon (2000) Riske Lemmens Mantra Publishing	*Eddie and Teddie* (1991) Gus Clarke Little Mammoth	*Finding the Greenstone* (1991) Alice Walker Hodder & Stoughton
	Mr Cool (1999) Hildegard Muller Cat's Whiskers	*Giant Hiccups* (1994) Jacqui Farley Tamarind	*The Iron Man* (2001) Ted Hughes Faber Children's Books
	Pumpkin Soup (1998) Helen Cooper Doubleday	*Green Eggs and Ham* (1980) Dr Seuss Picture Lions	*The Iron Woman* (1994) Ted Hughes Faber & Faber
	Snap-Happy Annie (1999) June Crebbin Puffin Books	*Jamaica and Brianna* (1995) Juanita Havill Heinemann/Mammoth	*The Selfish Giant* (1982) Oscar Wilde Puffin Books
		Jane and the Dragon (2000) Martin Baynton Walker Books	*War and Peas* (1974) Michael Foreman Hamish Hamilton
		Lucy's Quarrel (1997) Jennifer Northway Scholastic	
		The Rabbit Who Couldn't Say No (2000) Elena Goldoni Siphano Picture Books	
		Tusk, Tusk (1978) David Mckee Arrow Books	
Non-fiction		*Kosovan Journeys* (2001)* Howard Davies and Jill Rutter Refugee Council	*The School Council: A Children's Guide* (1999) Save the Children
			Bullies and Gangs (1996) Julie Johnson Franklin Watts

Resources for teachers

Social justice and equity

Activities and resources	■ *Education for Citizenship: Ideas into Action* (2001) N. Clough and C. Holden, Routledge and Falmer (KS2/P4–P7) ■ *Education for Development – A Teacher's Resources for Global Learning* (1995) Susan Fountain, Hodder & Stoughton/UNICEF (KS2/P4–P7) ■ *Our World, Our Rights: Teaching about Rights and Responsibilities in the Primary School* (1996)* Margo Brown (ed.), Amnesty International (KS1/P1–P3, KS2/P4–P7) ■ *Partners in Rights: Creative Activities Exploring Rights and Citizenship for 7–11-year-olds* (2000)* Save the Children (KS2/P4–P7) ■ *Refugees: A Resource Book for Primary Schools* (1998)* Jill Rutter, Refugee Council (KS1/P1–P3, KS2/P4–P7) ■ Series of pamphlets on Water, Food, Fair Trade, Transport and Waste and Recycling, Reading International Solidarity Centre (RISC) and Humanities Education Centre, Tower Hamlets (see DEC contacts) (KS1/P1–P3, KS2/P4–P7)
Additional resources	■ *The Paper Bag Game* (1995)* Christian Aid, age 9+, simulation game (KS2/P4–P7) ■ *Children First** six-poster set on everyday activities, Oxfam (KS1/P1–P3, KS2/P4–P7)
Websites for use by children (with adult support)	www.citizenship-pieces.org.uk www.oxfam.org.uk/coolplanet www.childrens-express.org
Background information for teachers	■ *Developing a Global Dimension in the School Curriculum* (2000) Department for Education and Employment ■ *Essential Learning for Everyone* (1999)* Colm Regan and Scott Sinclair, Birmingham DEC and 80:20 Ireland ■ *The Global Dimension in the Curriculum* (2001) Learning and Teaching Scotland ■ *The Human Rights Reader* (1997) Micheline R. Ishay, Routledge
	■ *In Safe Hands* (2001)* Save the Children ■ *Learning from Experience: World Studies in the Primary Curriculum* (1993) Miriam Steiner, Trentham Books ■ *The Stephen Lawrence Inquiry: Report of an Inquiry by Sir William MacPherson of Cluny* (1999) The Stationery Office ■ *Supporting Refugee Children in 21st Century Britain* (2001)* Jill Rutter, Trentham Books ■ *Values and Visions: Spiritual Development and Global Awareness in the Primary School* (1995)* S. Burns and G. Lamont, Manchester DEP in association with Hodder & Stoughton

Globalisation and interdependence

Activities and resources	■ *The Big City Pack* (1994)* C. Kelly et al, Oxfam (KS1/P1–P3, KS2/P4–P7)
	■ *Cairo: Four Children and their City* (1994)* D. Theodore and A. Grunsell, Oxfam (KS2/P4–P7)
	■ *The Clothes Line* (1998) T. Garlake, Oxfam (KS2/P4–7)
	■ *DIY Local–Global Guide* (2001) D. Richards, Reading International Solidarity Centre (RISC) (KS1/P1–P3, KS2/P4–P7)
	■ *Mapping Our World* (2000)* B. Ashmore, Oxfam (KS2/P4–P7)
	■ *Talking Drum* (1996)* R. Smillie Christian Aid/Save the Children Fund (Foundation Stage, Pre-5 and Early Years)
	■ *This Earth for Us* (2000)* Commonwealth Institute (English/Welsh and Scottish editions available) (KS1/P1–P3, KS2/P4–P7)
	■ *Toying with Technology* (2000)* M. Patience et al, Scottish DEC/Oxfam (KS1/P1–P3)
	■ *Woven Lives* (2001)* MUNDI (KS2/P4–P7)
Additional resources	■ *Market Place*,* Traidcraft, age 7–11, simulation game (KS2/P4–P7)
	■ *World Maps**
Websites for use by children (with adult support)	www.wateraid.org.uk/game
	www.yptenc.org.uk
Background information for teachers	■ *A Quick Guide to North–South School Links* (2001)* Leeds DEC
	■ *The A–Z of World Development* (1999)* Wayne Ellwood (ed.), New Internationalist Publications Ltd (also available as a CD ROM)
	■ *No Logo* (2000) Naomi Klein, Harper Collins
	■ *School Linking across the World. A Directory of Agencies Supporting North–South Linking* (2000) Shanda Leather, The Central Bureau for Educational Visits and Exchanges
	■ *The State of the World's Children* (2001) UNICEF
	■ *UNDP Human Development Report* (2001) Human Development Report Office (HDRO), UNDP
	■ *Material World: A Global Family* (1994) P. Menzel, Sierra Club Books
	■ *Eliminating World Poverty: Making Globalisation Work for the Poor* (2000) White Paper on International Development, Crown Copyright
	■ *An International Outlook: Educating Young Scots About the World* (2001) Scottish Executive

Appreciation of diversity

Activities and resources	■ *Your World, My World* (2001)* T. Garlake, Oxfam (Foundation Stage, Pre-5 and Early Years, KS1/ P1–P3, KS2/P4–P7)
	■ *Families* (1999)* Save the Children/Leeds DEC (Foundation Stage, Pre-5 and Early Years, KS1/ P1–P3, KS2/P4–P7)
	■ *Jamaica: Out of Many, One People* (2000)* Birmingham DEC (KS2/P4–P7)
	■ *Making Music on the Line* (2000)* Ken Patterson (ed.), Folkworks (video, CD and book) (KS2/P4–P7)
	■ *Toys and Tales with Everyday Materials* (1999)* Sudarshan Khanna, Gita Wolf, Anushka Ravi Shankar, Tara Publishing and National Institute of Design
Additional resources	■ *Wake Up World!* (CD ROM) (2000)* Anglia Multimedia
Websites for use by children (with adult support)	www.britkid.org www.pupsclub.org.uk
Background information for teachers	■ *Evaluating Artefacts* (1992)* Centre for Multicultural Education (Foundation Stage, Pre-5 and Early Years, KS1/ P1–P3, KS2/P4–P7)
	■ *Learning for All: Standards for Racial Equality in Schools* (2000) Commission for Racial Equality
	■ *Roots of the Future: Ethnic Diversity in the Making of Britain* (1996) Mayerline Frow, Commission for Racial Equality
	■ *Survival* background sheets on indigenous peoples (1998) Survival International
	■ *Teaching Racism or Tackling It?* (1999) Russell Jones, Trentham Books
	■ *Bangladeshi Children in our Schools: A Guide for Teachers* (1999)* HEC

Sustainable development

Activities and resources	■ *Citizenship for the Future: A Practical Classroom Guide* (2000)* David Hicks, WWF-UK (KS2/P4–P7)
	■ *Making a Difference* (2001)* D. Brinn, C. Fowler and C. Hester, RSBP/Oxfam (KS2/P4–P7)
	■ *Making it Happen, Agenda 21 and Schools* (1998)* Gillian Symons, WWF-UK (KS2/P4–P7)
	■ *Talking to the Earth* (1995) Gordon MacLellan, Capall Bann Publishing (Foundation Stage, Pre-5 and Early Years, KS1/ P1–P3, KS2/P4–P7)
	■ *Thengapalli* (1997)* D. Theodore, Hampshire CC Education/Hampshire DEC (KS2/P4–P7)
	■ *Waking Up* (2000)* Ballin et al, Birmingham DEC (KS2/P4–P7)
Additional resources	■ *Sowing and Harvesting* (1998)* Oxfam Education. (Simulation game) (KS2/P4–P7)
	■ *Making Compost at School* (2001) Royal Horticultural Society (KS1/P1–P3, KS2/P4–P7)

Continued overleaf

Sustainable development continued

Websites for use by children (with adult support)	www.funergy.org.uk www.dubble.co.uk
Background information for teachers	■ *A Safer Journey to School* (1999) Transport 2000 and DfEE ■ *Atlas of Earthcare* (1996)* Miles Litvinoff, Young Gaia ■ *The Community Tourism Guide* (2000)* Mark Mann for Tourism Concern, Earthscan Publications Ltd ■ *Education for Sustainable Development* (2001) Learning and Teaching Scotland ■ *Geography and the New Agenda: PSHE and Sustainable Development in the Primary Curriculum* (2000)* Keith Grimwade (ed.) Geographical Association ■ *Reframing the Early Childhood Curriculum: Educational Imperatives for the Future* (2000) Jane Page, Routledge ■ Sustainable Development Education Panel: First Annual Report (1999) DETR ■ *All Our Futures: Creativity, Culture and Education* (1999) DfEE/Crown Copyright, National Advisory Committee on Creative and Cultural Education

Peace and conflict resolution

Activities and resources	■ *Building Peace where I Live* (2000) National Peace Council (available from Pax Christi) (KS2/P4–P7) ■ *Developing Circle Time* (1995) Teresa Bliss, George Robinson and Barbara Maines, Lucky Duck Publishing Ltd (Foundation Stage, Pre-5 and Early Years, KS1/ P1–P3, KS2/P4–P7) ■ *Games, Games, Games 3* (1998)* The Woodcraft Folk (KS1/P1–P3, KS2/P4–P7) ■ *Parachute Games* (1992)* Peace Pledge Union (Foundation Stage, Pre-5 and Early Years, KS1/ P1–P3, KS2/P4–P7) ■ *Playground Peacemakers: Peaceful Conflict Resolution for Schools Using the Mediation Way for Teachers in KS1* (2000) Lorna Farrington (also available for KS2) ■ *Turn Your School Round* (1993) Jenny Mosley, LDA (Foundation Stage, Pre-5 and Early Years, KS1/P1–P3; KS2/P4–P7)
Additional resources	■ *Once Upon a Conflict* (1995)* T. Leindorfer, Pax Christi (Role Play Scenarios) ■ *The Two Mules*, Quaker Peace & Social Witness (poster)
Websites for use by children (with adult support)	www.citizenship-pieces.org.uk www.bullying.co.uk
Background information for teachers	■ *Building Blocks for Global Learning* (1999)* Ben Ballin and Helen Griffin (eds), Global Education Derby ■ *Changing our School* (1997) Highfield Junior School, Hodder ■ *Let's Mediate* (1997) Hilary Stacey and Pat Robinson, Lucky Duck Publishing ■ *Time for Peace* (1999) Janet Ganguli, Small Worlds Publications ■ *Thinking Together: Philosophical Inquiry for the Classroom* (1995) Philip Cam, Primary English Teaching Association and Hale & Iremonger

Books for initial teacher education

- *Development Education within Initial Teacher Training: Shaping a Better Future* (1997)* Sally Inman and Ros Wade, Oxfam
- *Daring to be a Teacher* (1990) Robin Richardson, Trentham Books
- *Developing the Global Teacher: Theory and Practice in Initial Teacher Education* (1996)* Miriam Steiner, Trentham Books

Whole-school resources

- *The Heart of the Matter* (1995) Scottish Consultancy Council on the Curriculum
- *Personal and Social Development 5–14 Exemplification: The Whole School Approach: A Staff Development Workshop* (1995) Scottish Consultancy Council on the Curriculum
- *The School is Us: A Practical Guide to Successful Whole School Change* (1993) WWF-UK and Manchester DEP

Periodicals and newsletters

Title	Publisher	Telephone
CEE Mail (sustainable development)	Council for Environmental Education	0118 950 2550
DEA Journal (development education)	Development Education Association	020 7490 8108
Developments	Department for International Development	0845 300 4100
Ethical Consumer	ECRA Publishing Ltd	0161 226 2929
Global Citizenship Link Bulletin (global citizenship issues)	Oxfam Education	020 7931 7660
Global Eye (general development issues)	Worldaware	020 8763 2555
Human Rights Education Newsletter	Quaker Peace and Social Witness	020 7663 1087
New Internationalist (general development issues)	New Internationalist	01858 439616
Orbit (general development issues)	Voluntary Services Overseas	020 8780 7500
Resurgence (green and environmental issues)	Resurgence	01208 841824

Contacts

The following organisations provide advice, information and teaching materials for primary level. Some may also offer talks and in-service training in schools. Please note that this is only a small selection of organisations, but covering as wide a range of issues as possible to reflect the issues highlighted in the Handbook.

Action Aid

Action Aid's vision is a world without poverty, in which every person can exercise their right to a life of dignity.
Hamlyn House
Macdonald Road
London, N19 5PG
Tel: 020 7561 7561
www.actionaid.org

Adopt-A-Minefield UK

Helps save lives by raising funds for mine clearance and survivor assistance and by raising awareness about the landmine problem.
59 Mansell Street
London, E1 8AN
Tel: 020 7265 4945
www.landmines.org.uk

Amnesty International

Works worldwide to promote human rights, for the release of prisoners of conscience, fair trials for political prisoners and an end to torture, political killings, 'disappearances' and the death penalty.
99–119 Rosebery Avenue
London, EC1R 4RE
Tel: 020 7814 6200
www.amnesty.org.uk

Anti-Slavery International

Works for the elimination of all forms of slavery in the world today.
Thomas Clarkson House
The Stableyard
Broomgrove Road
London, SW9 9TL
Tel: 020 7501 8920
www.antislavery.org

British Red Cross Society

Cares for people in crisis and works with local communities to help prepare them for potential emergencies.
9 Grosvenor Crescent
London, SW1W 9EJ
Tel: 020 7235 5454
www.redcross.org.uk

Wales
Third floor
Baltic House
Mount Stuart Square
Cardiff Bay, CF10 5FH
Tel: 029 2081 0021

Scotland
Alexandra House
204 Bath Street
Glasgow, G2 4HL
Tel: 0141 332 9591

Catholic Fund for Overseas Development (CAFOD)

Provides resources and INSET to support teachers in developing active global citizenship
Romero Close
Stockwell Road
London, SW9 9TY
Tel: 020 7733 7900
www.cafod.org.uk/schools.htm

Scottish Catholic Development Aid Fund (SCIAF)
19 Park Circus
Glasgow, G3 6BE

CAFOD Wales
11 Richmond Road
Cardiff, CF24 3AQ
Tel: 029 2045 3360

The Centre for Alternative Technology

Demonstrates globally sustainable technologies: wind, water and solar power, organic growing, and building design. Offers visits for schools, courses and publications.
Machynlleth
Powys, SY20 9AZ
Tel: 01654 703605
(education enquiries)
www.cat.org.uk

Christian Aid

Christian Aid provides resources and support for UK schools, enabling them to explore issues of Global Citizenship and to develop the skills to identify and take appropriate relevant action for a just global society.
35 Lower Marsh
London, SE1 7RT
Tel: 020 7620 4444

Scotland
41 George IV Bridge
Edinburgh, EH1 1EL
Tel: 0131 220 1254

Wales
Cymorth Cristnogol:
Contact Cardiff office for regional offices.
27 Church Road
Whitchurch
Cardiff, CF14 2DX
Tel: 029 20614435
www.christian-aid.org.uk
www.globalgang.org.uk

Comic Relief

Provides free curriculum resources to support teaching around issues behind Red Nose Day, e.g. Fair Trade, race.
5th Floor
89 Albert Embankment
London, SE1 7TP
Tel: 020 7820 5555
www.comicrelief.org.uk

Commission for Racial Equality

A non-governmental body that tackles racial discrimination and promotes racial equality.
Elliot House
10/12 Allington Street
London, SW1E 5EH
Tel: 020 7828 7022

Wales
14th Floor
Capital Tower
Greyfriars Street
Cardiff, CF1 3AG
Tel: 029 2038 8977

Scotland
Hanover House
45–51 Hanover Street
Edinburgh, EH2 2PJ
Tel: 0131 240 2600
www.cre.gov.uk

Commonwealth Institute

Focuses on expanding cultural horizons by working with young people on diversity, Global Citizenship and the modern Commonwealth through providing printed and on-line resources.
Kensington High Street
London, W8 6NQ
Tel: 020 7603 4535
www.commonwealth.org.uk

Council for Environmental Education

Works to ensure that the principles of sustainable development are at the heart of education policy and practice.
94 London Street
Reading, RG1 4SJ
Tel: 0118 950 2550
www.cee.org.uk

CREATE

A government organisation that coordinates and promotes energy education at all levels in the UK.
Kenley House
25 Bridgeman Terrace
Wigan, WN1 1TD
Tel: 01942 322271
www.create.org.uk

Earth Centre

An educational visitor centre that aims to inspire understanding of sustainable development
Denaby Main
Doncaster, DN12 4EA
Tel: 01709 513915
www.earthcentre.org.uk

Eco-Schools

A Europe wide project designed to encourage and acknowledge whole school action for the environment. Eco-schools is both a programme and an award scheme.
Contact: Tidy Britain Group
Eco-Schools
Elizabeth House
The Pier
Wigan, WN3 4EX
Tel: 01942 612621
www.eco-schools.org.uk

Fairtrade Foundation

Ensures a better deal for small-scale producers and awards a consumer label, the Fairtrade mark, to products which meet internationally recognised standards of Fair Trade.
Suite 204
16 Baldwin's Gardens
London, EC1N 7RJ
Tel: 020 7405 5942
www.fairtrade.org.uk

Wales
Wales Fairtrade Forum
c/o Christian Aid in Wales

Free Tibet Campaign

An independent organisation campaigning for Tibetans' fundamental human rights to be respected and an end to the Chinese occupation of Tibet.
1 Rosoman Place
London, EC1R 0JY
Tel: 020 7833 9958
www.freetibet.org

Friends of the Earth

An international network of environmental pressure groups, with a wide network of local campaigning groups.
26–28 Underwood Street
London, N1 7JQ
Tel: 020 7490 1555

Global Citizenship: The Handbook for Primary Teaching

Wales
10 Llandaff Road
Canton
Cardiff, CF11 9NJ
Tel: 029 2022 2066

Scotland
72 Newhaven Road
Edinburgh, EH6 5QG
Tel: 0131 554 9977
www.foe.co.uk

Geographical Association

Aims to further the study and teaching of geography

160 Selly Street
Sheffield, S1 4BF
Tel: 0114 296 0088
www.geography.org.uk

Going for Green

A national environmental awareness campaign based around the promotion of the Green Code, which reinforces the idea of sustainable development and encourages action.

Elizabeth House
The Pier
Wigan, WN3 4EX
Tel: 01942 612621

Wales
33–35 Cathedral Road
Cardiff, CF1 9NB
Tel: 029 2025 6700

Scotland
Forward Scotland
c/o Scottish Power
St Vincent's Crescent
Glasgow
Tel: 0141 227 7684
www.gfg.iclnet.org.uk
www.tidybritain.org.uk

Greenpeace

Undertakes campaigning work from promoting solutions, to direct actions, political lobbying and scientific research.

Canonbury Villas
London, N1 2PN
Tel: 020 7865 8100
www.greenpeace.org.uk

The Guide Dogs for the Blind Association

Provide information for teachers and pupils on issues of blindness and the work of guide dogs

Hillfields
Burghfield Common
Reading, RG7 3YG
Tel: 0870 600 2323
www.guidedogs.org.uk

Intermediate Technology Group (ITDG)

ITDG provides information and resources for teachers on the issue of sustainable development, using case studies from both northern and southern hemispheres.

Schumacher Centre for Technology and Development
Bourton Hall
Bourton-on-Dunsmore
Rugby, CV23 9Q2
Tel: 01926 634400
www.itdg.org

Local Government Association

For information about local Agenda 21 initiatives in England and Wales call
020 7664 3000
www.lga.gov.uk

Wales
Local Government House
Drake Walk
Cardiff, CF10 4LG
Tel: 029 2046 8600
www.wlga.gov.uk

Scotland
Rosebery House
Haymarket Street
Edinburgh, EH12 5XZ
Tel: 0131 474 9200

Minority Rights Group

An international non-governmental organization working to secure rights for ethnic, religious and linguistic minorities and indigenous peoples worldwide, and to promote co-operation between communities.

379 Brixton Rd
London, SW9 7DE
Tel: 020 7978 9498
www.minorityrights.org

The National Botanic Garden of Wales

Committed to promoting a sustainable approach to the environment through the ethics and practice of creating a national botanic garden.

Middleton Hall
Llanarthne
Carmarthen, SA32 8HG
Tel: 01558 668768
www.gardenofwales.org.uk

The National Deaf Children's Society

An organisation of families, parents and carers that exists to enable deaf children and young people to maximise their skills and development

15 Dufferin Street
London, EC1Y 8UR
Helpline: 020 7250 0123
(England, Scotland and Wales)
www.ndcs.org.uk

Native American Educational Trust

Dedicated to the promotion of Native American history and cultures through storytelling and provision of materials.

21 Little Preston St
Brighton, BN1 2HQ
Tel: 01273 328357

New Economics Foundation

A think-tank working towards a just and equitable economy centred on people and the environment.

Cinnamon House
6/8 Cole Street
London, SE1 4YH
Tel: 020 7407 7447
www.neweconomics.org

National Society for the Prevention of Cruelty to Children (NSPCC)

Specialises in child protection and the prevention of cruelty to children.

NSPCC National Centre
42 Curtain Road
London, EC2A 3NH
Tel: 020 7825 2500
www.nspcc.org.uk

One World Week

Enabling people to learn about, act on, and raise awareness of global issues.

PO Box 2555
Reading, RG1 4XW
Tel: 0118 939 4933
www.oneworldweek.org

The Permaculture Association of Britain

Supports people and projects through training, networking and research, using the ethics and principles of permaculture.

BCM Permaculture Association
London, WC1N 3XX
Tel: 07041 390170
www.permaculture.org.uk

Quaker Peace & Social Witness

The Peace Education Advisory Programme of Quaker Peace & Social Witness encourages peace education within schools nationally, exploring issues such as human rights, citizenship and social justice, and promoting skills of conflict resolution, mediation and problem solving.

Friends House
Euston Rd
London, NW1 2BJ
Tel: 020 7663 1087
www.quaker.org.uk

Refugee Council

Gives help and support to refugees and asylum seekers arriving and surviving in Britain.

Refugee Help and Support Team
3 Bondway
London, SW8 1SJ
Tel: 020 7820 3000
www.refugeecouncil.org.uk

Wales
Wales Refugee Council
Unit 8 Williams Court
Trade Street
Cardiff, CF1 5DG
Tel: 029 2066 6250

Royal National Institute for the Blind (RNIB)

Provides information, support and advice for anyone with a serious sight problem or for those working with them.

224 Great Portland Street
London, W1W 5AA
Helpline: 08457 669999

Wales
Trident Court
East Moors Road
Cardiff, CF24 5TD
Tel: 029 2045 0440

Scotland
Dunedin House
25 Ravelston Terrace
Edinburgh, EH4 3TP
Tel: 0131 311 8500
www.rnib.org.uk

Royal Society for the Protection of Birds (RSPB)

Provides a range of classroom resources suitable for primary and secondary teachers. All are linked to the new UK National Curricula.

Education Department
The Lodge
Sandy
Bedfordshire, SG19 2DL
Tel: 01767 680551

Wales
Sutherland House
Castlebridge
Cowbridge Road East
Cardiff, CF11 9AB
Tel: 029 2035 3000

Scotland
Dunedin House
25 Ravelston Terrace
Edinburgh, EH4 3TP
Tel: 0131 311 6500
www.rspb.co.uk

Royal Society for the Prevention of Cruelty to Animals (RSPCA)

Campaigns on a variety of welfare issues affecting animals in the UK and throughout the world.

Wilberforce Way
Southwater
Horsham
West Sussex, RH13 9RS
Tel: 0870 3335 999
www.rspca.org.uk

RUGMARK UK

Works to eradicate illegal child labour in the South Asian carpet industry through factory monitoring, product labelling and education of former child labourers.

Thomas Clarkson House
The Stableyard
Broomgrove Road
London, SW9 9TL
Tel: 020 7737 2675
www.rugmark.org

Runnymede Trust
UK-based think tank on ethnicity and cultural diversity. Challenges racial discrimination and aims to influence anti-racist legislation.
Suite 106
The London Fruit and Wool Exchange
London, E1 6EP
Tel: 020 7377 9222
www.runnymedetrust.org.uk

Sapere
The society for the advancement of philosophical enquiry and reflection in education.
7 Cloister Way
Leamington Spa, CV32 6QE
Tel: 01925 423612
www.sapere.net

Save the Children UK
Works with schools and youth groups in the UK to promote children's rights in the context of Global Citizenship through the production of resources, websites and outreach programmes.
17 Grove Lane
London, SE5 8RD
Tel: 020 7703 5400

Wales
Phoenix House
2nd Floor
8 Cathedral Road
Cardiff, CF1 9LJ
Tel: 029 2039 6838

Scotland
2nd Floor
Haymarket House
8 Clifton Terrace
Edinburgh, EH12 5DR
Tel: 0131 527 8207
www.savethechildren.org.uk

School Councils UK
A training and support agency in the area of school and class councils, working with teachers and pupils to set up effective structures for pupil involvement.
57 Etchingham Park Road
Finchley
London, N3 2EB
Tel: 020 8349 2459
www.schoolcouncils.org

SCOPE
A national disability organisation whose focus is people with cerebral palsy; works to achieve equality and civil rights for disabled people.
PO Box 833
Milton Keynes
MK12 5NY
Tel: 0808 800 3333

Wales
Wales Partnership Area Office
The Wharf
Schooner Way
Cardiff, CF10 4EU
Tel: 029 2046 1703
www.scope.org.uk

Sight Savers
An organisation which combats blindness and provides services to blind people in Majority World countries through working with local partners.
Grosvenor Hall
Bolnore Road
Haywards Heath
West Sussex, RH16 4BX
Tel: 01444 446600
www.sightsavers.org.uk

Survival International
A worldwide organisation supporting tribal peoples.
6 Charterhouse Buildings
Goswell Road
London, EC1M 7ET
Tel: 020 7687 8700
www.survival.org.uk

Teacher's Advisory Council on Alcohol and Drug Education (TACADE)
Provides support for those working to improve the health of children and young people.
1 Hulme Place
The Crescent
Salford, M5 4QA
Tel: 0161 745 8925
www.tacade.com

Tourism Concern
Raises awareness and concern for the impact from tourism on communities and the environment, both in the UK and worldwide.
Stapleton House
277–281 Holloway Rd
London, N7 8HN
Tel: 0207 533 3330
www.tourismconcern.org.uk

Traidcraft
Works to promote fair trading systems as a solution to majority world poverty.
Communications Section
Traidcraft PLC
Kingsway
Gateshead, NE11 0NE
Tel: 0191 491 0591
www.traidcraft.co.uk

Wales
10 Llandaff Road
Canton
Cardiff, CF11 9NJ
Tel: 029 2022 2066

United Nations Association
Campiagning and educating to turn the ideals of the UN into reality.
3 Whitehall Court
London
SW1A 2EL
Tel: 020 7930 2931

Wales
Welsh Centre for International Affairs
Temple of Peace
Cathays Park
Cardiff, CF1 3AP
Tel: 029 2022 8549
www.una-uk.org

United Nations Children's Fund (UNICEF)
Has regionally based Education Officers covering England, Wales, Scotland and Northern Ireland who run free INSET sessions on how to integrate the Convention on the Rights of the Child into the Citizenship curriculum.
Africa House
64–78 Kingsway
London, WC2B 6NB
Tel: 020 7405 5592
www.unicef.org.uk

The United Nations High Commissioner for Refugees (UNHCR)
An international humanitarian organisation mandated by the United Nations to lead and coordinate global action to safeguard the rights and well-being of refugees.
Millbank Tower
21–24 Millbank
London, SW1P 4PQ
Tel: 020 7932 1022
www.unhcr.ch

War on Want
Campaigns against the causes of poverty and helps the dispossessed fight back.
Campaign Against World Poverty
Fenner Brockway House
37–39 Great Guildford Street
London, SE1 0ES
Tel: 020 7620 1111
www.waronwant.org

Waste Watch
Practical action on waste reduction, reuse and recycling, including organising trips to recycling centres for schools and promoting links between school and community waste projects.
96 Tooley Street
London, SE1 2TH
Tel: 020 7089 2100

For general recycling enquiries ring the Waste Watch wasteline on:
0870 243 0136
www.wastewatch.org.uk

Wateraid
A development charity working through partner organisations to improve domestic water supply, sanitation and associated hygiene practices in the Majority World.
Prince Consort House
27–29 Albert Embankment
London, SE1 7UB
Tel: 020 7793 4500
www.wateraid.org.uk

Worldaware
UK-based organisation that works to raise awareness of international development issues, and provides curriculum-based materials and advice for schools.
Echo House
Ullswater Crescent
Coulsdon
Surrey, CR5 2HR
Tel: 020 8763 2555
www.worldaware.org.uk
www.globaleye.org.uk

World Links and Partnerships at the Education and Training Group of the British Council
World Links and Partnerships is a division of the British Council which promotes school linking with Majority World countries to enrich understanding of development issues.
World Links and Partnerships at the Central Bureau
10 Spring Gardens
London, SW1A 2BN
Tel: 020 7389 4004

Wales
28 Park Place
Cardiff, CF1 3QE
Tel: 029 2039 7346

Scotland
3 Bruntfield Crescent
Edinburgh, EH10 4HD
Tel: 0131 447 8024
www.wotw.org.uk

World Wide Fund for Nature (WWF)
Campaigns for the protection of endangered spaces and species, and addresses global threats.
Panda House
Weyside Park
Godalming
Surrey, GU7 1XR
Tel: 01483 426444

Wales
Room 3
13 Baltic House
Mount Stuart Square
Cardiff, CF10 5FH
Tel: 029 204 54970

Scotland
8 The Square
Aberfeldy
Perthshire, PH15 2BB
Tel: 01887 820449
www.wwf-uk.org
www.wwflearning.co.uk

Additional support for Citizenship in primary schools

The Centre for Citizenship Studies in Education

University of Leicester
School of Education
21 University Road
Leicester, LE1 7RF
Tel: 0116 252 3681
www.le.ac.uk/education/centres/citizenship

Citizenship Foundation

Ferroners House
Shaftesbury Place
Aldersgate Street
London, EC2Y 8AA
Tel: 020 7367 0500
www.citfou.org.uk

Council for Education in World Citizenship

CEWC Cymru
Temple of Peace
Cathays Park
Cardiff, CF10 3AP
Tel: 029 202 28549
www.cewc-cymru.org.uk

Institute for Citizenship

Queensbridge Building
Hackney Professional Development Centre
Albion Drive
London E8 4ET
Tel: 020 7241 7414
www.citizen.org.uk

Development Education Centres

Listed below are Development Education Centres (DECs) and other resources centres offering professional support to teachers and youth workers. They are divided by country and then listed in alphabetical order by town/city. The highlighted entries are umbrella organisations for development education in that country. Email addresses follow the phone numbers.

England

Development Education Association

29–31 Cowper Street
London EC2A 4AP
020 7490 8108
devedassoc@gn.apc.org

Cumbria Development Education Centre

Kelsick Annexe
St. Martin's College
Ambleside, Cumbria
LA22 9BB
015394 30231
cdec@ucsm.ac.uk

Aylesbury Development Education Centre

Elmhurst Middle School
Dunsham Lane
Aylesbury, Bucks
HP20 2DB
01296 395185
adec@nildram.co.uk

Pestalozzi International Development Education Centre

Pestalozzi Children's Village Trust, Sedlescombe
Battle, East Sussex
TN33 0RR
01424 870444
dec@mistral.co.uk

Tide, Development Education Centre (Birmingham)

Gillett Centre
998 Bristol Road, Selly Oak
Birmingham B29 6LE
0121 472 3255
info@tidec.org

Development Education in Dorset

Slades Farm School
Ensbury Avenue
Bournemouth BH10 4HG
01202 532484
deed@gn.apc.org

Brighton Peace and Environment Centre

One World Library and Education Unit
43 Gardener Street
Brighton, East Sussex
BN1 1UN
01273 620128
bripeace@pavilion.co.uk

Cambridge Centre for Development and Environment Education

The Harambee Centre,
Emmanuel United Reformed Church
(Opposite Pembroke College)
Trumpington Street
Cambridge CB2 1RR
01223 358116
harambee@dial.pipex.com

World Education Development Group

98a Broad Street
Canterbury CT1 2LU
01227 766552
wedg@freeuk.com

Carlisle One World Centre

Church of Scotland,
Chapel Street
Carlisle CA1 1JA
01228 546286
owccarlisle@surfaid.org

Gloucestershire Development Education Centre

30 St George's Place
Cheltenham GL50 3JZ
01242 224311
glos.dec@virgin.net

Cheshire Development Education Centre

Campbell Community Hall,
Boughton
Chester CH3 5BR
01244 347880
cheshire_dec@hotmail.com

Traders Fair DEC

Traders Fair World Shop
4 Portal Precinct
Sir Isaac's Walk
Colchester, Essex CO1 1JJ
01206 763380
foxnorth@tinyworld.co.uk

Worldaware

Echo House, Ullswater Crescent
Coulsdon, Surrey CR5 2HR
020 8763 2555
education@worldaware.org.uk

Devon Development Education

Queen Elizabeth Community College
Upper School
Western Road
Crediton, Devon EX17 3LU
01363 776515
devondeved@iname.com

Derby Rainbow Centre

88 Abbey Street
Derby DE22 3SQ
01332 298185
derbyrainbow@derbyrainbow.f9.co.uk

Oxfam Development Education

96 South Street
Exeter EX1 1EN
01392 253 241
exetereducation@oxfam.org.uk

Hull Development Education Centre

Room 29,
Hull Education Centre
Coronation Road North
Hull HU5 5RL
01482 616619
dec@dechull.karoo.co.uk

Global Link

18 China Street
Lancaster, Lancs LA1 1EX
01524 36201
globallink@gn.apc.org

Leeds DEC

Roundhay Resources Centre
233-237 Roundhay Road
Leeds LS8 4HS
0113 380 5655
anything@leedsdec.demon.co.uk

Leicestershire Development Education Centre

The Seed Store, Leicester University Botanic Garden
Stoughton Drive
South Oadby
Leicester LE2 2NE
0116 271 2933

Liverpool World Centre

St James Community Centre, Nelson Street
Liverpool L1 5DN
salevans@hotmail.com

Oxfam Development Education

4th Floor, 4 Bridge Place
London SW1V 1XY
020 7931 7660
vicdeved@oxfam.org.uk

Community Development and Advocacy Centre

Suite 51, Imperial House
64 Willowby Lane
London N17
020 8350 0684
zayayeebo@aol.com

London Development Education Centre

293-299 Kentish Town Road
London NW5 2TJ
020 7424 9525
londec@hotmail.com

Global Citizenship: The Handbook for Primary Teaching

Humanities Education Centre

Tower Hamlets PDC,
English Street
London E3 4TA
020 7364 6405
hec@gn.apc.org

Breakthrough Development Education Project

52 Fairlight Road, Tooting
London SW17 0JD
020 8767 5013
breakthroughchurch@
compuserve.com

Kent and the Wider World

60 Marsham Street
Maidstone, Kent ME14 1EW
01622 769282
kww@csr.org.uk

Malvern Development Education Centre

22 Church Street
Malvern, Worcestershire
WR14 2AY
01684 565796

Development Education Project (Manchester)

c/o Manchester
Metropolitan University
801 Wilmslow Road,
Didsbury
Manchester M20 8RG
0161 445 2495
depman@gn.apc.org

Wiltshire World Studies Centre

Marlborough Brandt Group
1A London Road
Marlborough SN8 1PH
01672 514078
mbguk@talk21.com

Teesside One World Centre

MacMillan College,
PO Box 8, Stockton Road
Middlesbrough TS5 4YU
01642 250930
teesoneworld@
tinyonline.co.uk

Global Ed MK (GEMK)

Saxon Hall,
Stantonbury Campus,
Stantonbury
Milton Keynes MK14 6BN
01908 310951
information@
mkwdec.org.uk

Norfolk Education and Action for Development

Third World Centre
38 Exchange Street
Norwich NR2 1AX
01603 610993
nead@gn.apc.org

MUNDI

Faculty of Education
Jubilee Campus
University of Nottingham
Nottingham NG8 1BB
0115 951 4485
kate.edmonds@
nottingham.ac.uk

Oxford Development Education Centre

East Oxford Community Centre,
Princes Street
Oxford OX4 1DD
01865 790490
odec@gn.apc.org

Lancashire Global Education Centre

37 St Peter's Square
Preston PR1 7BX
01772 252299
lgec@bigfoot.com

Reading International Solidarity Centre

35–39 London Street
Reading RG1 4PS
0118 958 6692
risc@risc.org.uk

South Yorkshire Development Education Centre

Woodthorpe School
Woodthorpe Road
Sheffield S13 8DD
0114 265 6662
decsy@gn.apc.org

Craven Development Education Centre

Tennant House, Malham
Skipton, North Yorkshire
BD23 4DA
01729 830372
d.howlett@bigfoot.com

Cornish Association for Development Education

C.A.D.E Centre, Penair
School, St Clements Hill
Truro TR1 1TN
01872 263233
cade@
cadecentre.free-online.co.uk

Hampshire Development Education Centre

Falcon House, Romsey Road
Winchester SO22 5PL
01962 856106
hampshire.dec@
btinternet.com

Global and Development Education Centre (GLADE)

Community Resource
Centre, 9 Garrett Road
Yeovil, Somerset BA20 2TJ
01935 433186
glade@gn.apc.org

Centre for Global Education

College of Rippon and York
Lord Mayors Walk
York YO31 7EX
01904 716839
global.ed@dial.pipex.com

Northern Ireland

One World Centre for Northern Ireland

4 Lower Crescent
Belfast BT7 1NR
028 9024 1879
belfastdec@gn.apc.org

Scotland

IDEAS

34–36 Rose Street,
North Lane
Edinburgh EH2 2NP
0131 225 5949
mail@
ideas.freeserve.co.uk

Montgomery Development Education Centre

120 Rosemount Place
Aberdeen AB25 2YW
01224 620111
mdec.abdn@virgin.net

Highland One World Group

Education Centre, Castle St
Dingwall, Rosshire
IV15 9HU
01381 621265
Janis.Keast@hcs.uhi.ac.uk

One World Centre (Dundee)

189 Princes Street
Dundee DD4 6DQ
01382 454603
deved@
oneworld1.freeserve.co.uk

Scottish Development Education Centre

34–36 Rose Street,
North Lane
Edinburgh EH2 2NP
0131 225 7617
mail@scotdec.org.uk

Oxfam Development Education

5th Floor, Fleming House,
134 Renfrew Street,
Glasgow G3 6ST
0141 331 1455
scotlandrg@oxfam.org.uk

Wales

Cyfanfyd

Temple of Peace
Cathays Park
Cardiff CF10 3AP
029 2022 8549
cyfanfyd@wcia.org.uk

Oxfam Development Education

Oxfam Cymru
46-48 Station Road,
Llanishen
Cardiff CF14 5LU
029 2075 7067
oxfamcymru@
oxfam.org.uk

World Education Project

School of Education,
Welsh National
Centre for RE
Normal Site
Bangor, Gwynedd LL57 2PX
01248 383728
eds038@bangor.ac.uk

Powys Environment and Development Education Centre

Unit G, Old Station
Workshops
Llanidloes, Powys SY18 6EB
01686 412731

Global Connections

2 Castle Terrace
Pembroke, Pembrokeshire
SA71 4LA
01646 687800
gcconnect@globalnet.co.uk